Ghosts in the Classroom

Stories of College Adjunct Faculty--
and the Price We All Pay

Edited by
Michael Dubson

Camel's Back Books
www.camelsbackbooks.com

Ghosts in the Classroom
ISBN: 0-9658977-1-0

Library of Congress Catalog Card Number: 00-92439

Camel's Back Books
Box 181126
Boston, Massachusetts 02118
www.camelsbackbooks.com

This book is dedicated to all those people who, loving their field and believing in the importance and power of learning, went into teaching with the highest of hopes and the best of intentions-- only to find themselves trapped in the adjunct track.

CONTENTS

Ghosts
in the
Classroom

No Place

People who make a profit off cattle
know how to manage capital. In my line
of work I'm expected to manage
without a desk and all the perks
that go with it. Telephone, stapler, paper
clips, space for coat and Bausch and Lomb
contact lens equipment: cleanser, sterile
wetting solution, face cloth, mascara,
tissues—an on-the-job-emergency
is complicated by make-up issues.
The question is how much can I carry
back and forth on the train and all day
in between? Classroom, bathroom, coffee cart,
print shop—you name the place and I'm schlepping
textbooks, hand-outs, student papers. Good thing
my back is broad, feet arched and uncomplaining
except in the wet or cold. But leaving
my house in boots or clodhoppers means
toting pumps in, travelers on site, absent
a spot to park them. Again, I ask you
how much can I carry? And don't answer
hey, it's the whining that's heavy. I've heard
it before, from my obstetrician who couldn't
tell twins from poormouth; they weighed in
at thirteen pounds. Most days my satchel
weighs more, though it's hard to be precise.
There's shame attached to having no place
that defies bromides or pep rallies,
which I hold in my head to muffle the sound
of cows lowing in milking sheds.

Cynthia Duda

Introduction: "A" Is for Adjunct, and Higher Education Flunks

During a routine spelling/grammar check of this collection, an ironically amusing event occurred. In several essays, some authors used the phrase "adjuncts who." The grammar checker consistently announced that one only uses "who" when referring to people. Adjuncts, according to a computer system, are not people. That sentiment is apparently shared by many others, as the following essays illustrate; one of the authors even titled her piece accordingly.

Adjunct faculty are the underclass of higher education: a combination of migrant workers, sweat shop staff and slaves. No one can justify and endorse such treatment without first dehumanizing the person doing the job. But there are many people behind the job. People with hopes and dreams, partners and children, problems and pain. According to statistics gathered by the National Education Association, there are 1,100,000 college and university teachers in the United States. Over half of them, approximately 560,000, are adjunct.

The use of adjunct faculty began innocently enough, as bad things often do. Members of the business community were initially brought in to teach highly specialized classes that academic faculty could not teach. The remuneration offered for this was minimal. The business person was successful in his/her field and didn't need the money. Instead, the primary gain for their efforts was a certain amount of prestige. The adjunct phenomenon was born.

Over the past three decades, changes in society and in the educational system—excessive tuition increases, changes in student demographics, budget shortfalls, hiring freezes, cuts in financial aid, a decline in public and private support for academic education, and a growing corporate mindset—caused an increasing reliance on adjunct faculty. Some of those adjunct faculty have continued to be careered people who teach on the side for extra money, prestige or both. Others are those who've retired from education, full-time homemakers or people who, for whatever reason, have some leisure time and are teaching for "fun." However, the largest group, the growing group, are the career adjuncts—people who have trained and prepared for careers in higher education and are seeking full employment. For many college teachers, becoming an adjunct first is now the only way in.

Today, there is a growing awareness of both the damage to educational quality and the psychological harm done to adjuncts because of the terms of the adjunct job. Consequently, adjunct faculty are organizing in record numbers to change the system. The voices you will hear in this book are from those people who have been in the trenches—in the classroom, in the battle—as adjuncts.

I am very grateful to the diverse, highly accomplished group of men and women who were willing to share their stories with the world. You will see how alike, and yet how different, each of the stories are. Many are full of pain and sadness; others full of rage. But even in the midst of pain or rage, there is still a belief in something bigger than a single person's situation. Sometimes, there is even humor.

The writers in this book have taught in two-year and four-year colleges, in the public and the private systems and in urban and rural schools. Every major geographical area of the United States is represented here. Some of these people have left the teaching profession for good, having had more than enough. Others are still slugging away in the adjunct track. Others have been fortunate enough to land full-time jobs, and yet, are still able to recall the anger, frustration or pain of their adjunct memories.

Many of the writers of these essays are victims. Others are villains. In all cases, the parameters of the adjunct job loom over them and their students and make a bad situation worse. Many of them are afraid, and their manuscripts were delivered with enormous amounts of trepidation, fear of the retribution and terrorism found only in academic departments. Because of that, a number of these writers are presenting their work under pseudonyms. In addition, if any person or place is named in an essay, the names are fabricated.

This anonymity is done to protect the privacy of the writers and the innocent. As well, it protects the privacy of the guilty. But the adjunct system is not simply a problem in one place; it is a systemic problem across higher education. No one is going to be able to say, "We don't treat our adjuncts like that here." Most of the stories in this book could have taken place at any school in this country.

One thing obvious about this collection is that there is an over-representation of English teachers. Perhaps this is because English teachers are more likely going to be writers and are more likely going to respond to a call for manuscripts. And perhaps it's because English is usually one of the largest departments of every college. And, with approximately 20-25 students per class and a plethora of writing assignments to evaluate each term, English is a labor intensive subject. It is in the labor intensive, as well as the introductory and developmental courses, where adjuncts work.

The essays in this book cover a great deal of adjunct territory. In "I Am an Adjunct" through "Will I Pass the Test?," the writers have eloquently, using moving and often shocking detail, presented the big picture on what life is like for the career adjunct. "We Only Come out at Night" and "Strange Fish" address clearly the double standards between full-time and part-time faculty, an idea that comes up in many of the other essays as well.

An enormous amount of what could be creative teaching energy is wasted in the resentment and contempt between part-time and full-time faculty. "The Lonely Run of the Adjunct Instructor" discusses the poor way adjuncts can be publicly treated, as well as showing how adjuncts are often encouraged, even expected to take on extra duties for free or for empty promises of more secure employment. In "Rock the Boat," the author discusses how and why adjuncts need to organize, and "The Censorship of Part-timers," "Adjunct Apartheid" and "Two Years, One Quarter" explains what can happen when adjunct faculty, particularly as individuals standing alone, do stand up for themselves. "Adjunct Misery," "The Witch and the Wimp," "From the Shade of the Tower," "Farewell to Matyora" and "Circles" all present examples of capricious adjunct firings or the game playing and circular reasoning used to deny long-term adjuncts full-time jobs, even one semester ones. "Professional" and "Stealth Justice" are two adjunct stories about academia's most severe crime--plagiarism (at this point in time, the poor treatment of adjuncts does not yet qualify). Both illustrate in very different ways how the parameters of adjunct employment negatively affect both student and teacher. "A Night in the Adjunct Life" and "Sit Down When Shots Are Fired!" are representative examples of the difficult situations that only adjunct faculty would be put into and expected to do well in. Finally, "A Lover's Complaint" and "Farewell to Teaching" are both from writers who, after more than giving it the old college try, vowed to leave the profession forever.

By the time you finish reading this book, you will know what anyone who has ever worked as an adjunct knows—some of the employment practices of higher education need a complete overhaul. No one else but the fast food industry allows so much of its principle work to be done by underpaid, expendable help. How many other professionals are hired on the spot and then expected to do an outstanding job without training or support? How many other professionals are expected to give selflessly of their time and mind for less than minimum wage, even expected to take on extra responsibilities for free?

No other profession but academia presents itself as the source of knowledge, the provider of educated personnel to all other professions, with the right and the ability to tell others what to think and how to think. The excessive use and abuse of adjuncts puts the grandstanding, the pontificating and the intellectualism of higher education officials into a very different light indeed.

Unfortunately, the trend in corporate American society in more and more professions is for more and more "adjunct" jobs (i.e. temporary, part-time, low paying, no benefits). That raises questions about the morality of that phenomena, and about the dignity and the rights of the people forced into those situations. In this book about adjunct employees in education, you will see how what may be gained in profit is lost in both the quality of service and the human dignity of the provider.

A college education remains for many an admission ticket. For many others, it remains the ultimate route of escape. It remains one of the few places in the world where open discussion and exploration of ideas is a legitimate and admirable experience (unless one is challenging adjunct employment policies). It is a wild, fascinating, crazy, exciting place—the maddest mix of the left and the right, of tedious drudgery and empowering freedom, of wild parties and of serious planning. The work that college teachers do is vital to the success of every student and to the survival of the system.

Fifty percent of all college teachers are adjunct. How many adjunct teachers are going into America's college classrooms angry, bitter, depressed, afraid, paranoid, burdened with major financial worries, perhaps seriously ill and uninsured, or just extremely overworked and scattered? What kind of teaching can such a person do? How does this kind of teacher positively affect his/her students? If they are able and willing to do the work for inadequate compensation, what then is good teaching worth?

I'm sure there are more than enough pompous college leaders who would say, between liberal platitudes, that they're not responsible for the choices the adjuncts make or for the mess they find themselves in after years of adjunct teaching. But the schools simply have no right to offer teaching jobs under these conditions. The system must change. There should be fewer adjuncts, better conditions for adjuncts and recognition, reward and reparation given to the hordes of adjuncts who have more than proven themselves over and over and over again.

If teaching college is a profession, then *all* the people doing that work needed to be treated as professionals, not just some of them. If teaching college is important work, then *all* people doing that work need to be given the resources and support to do that work well, not just some of them. If the money is not there to do this now, then education and government leaders need to get together to find it. If the money is there but the political will is not, then change will only happen if considerable external pressure is applied.

If teaching college is not a profession, or important work, then we need to stop lying to ourselves and to each other about what a college education is all about, and what is really going on in college classrooms.

After reading the essays in this book, you decide.

Michael Dubson
Boston
October, 2000

I Am an Adjunct

by M. Theodore Swift

I am an adjunct. I am a statistic of corruption. In a world where job security and employer loyalty have become a thing of the past, where people are working harder and longer and making less money, where the discrepancy between executive and worker pay is higher than ever, I roam the night a phantom, seeking recognition, subsistence, salvation. I know I'm not very likely to find it.

I am an adjunct. I am of the class of college and university faculty who, depending on who you talk to, aren't any good, really don't care, are smiled at with pity, or sneered at with contempt. I am a member of that class of faculty who, depending on the school, teaches anywhere from one-third to one-half—or more—of that school's course offerings. Yet, I am invisible. My name and degrees do not appear in the school catalogue, no matter how many years I have worked there. My name does not appear in the course catalogue next to the classes I will be teaching. I have no phone number, no office number, no office. I work on a semester contract, or a year's contract if I'm lucky, and receive, for the most part, no benefits. No matter how many years of continuous service at the school I have, I'm always treated as a temporary hire who can be cut loose at any moment, for any reason.

My work has allowed the schools I have worked for to stay open and functional. They have filled their classes with more people than their full-time teachers could ever teach. They have expanded their night schools, their summer programs, their intersession programs, their life-long learning outreaches because of me. They can fill my classes with huge numbers of students and reap tremendous profits. They can threaten me with unemployment or prorate my salary when my classes don't meet their (not all that) minimum figures.

I am an adjunct. I am an educated, intelligent, well-meaning person. I have the advanced degrees the colleges market as being the ticket to respect and financial security, although they do not respect nor financially reward mine. I have the same degree as the full-time faculty with whom I work, and I do the same work they do. Yet, I am treated so very differently.

I work half a semester before I ever see a dime. They get paychecks every week or every other week. The second half of my pay is held as blackmail until I turn in my grades, implying that I am not professional and cannot be trusted. If I teach eight courses in an academic year, I make approximately $16,000. They teach eight to ten courses during an academic year and make, on the average, $40,000. I must horde my money and pinch my pennies for I must live on it during the semester breaks. Full-time teachers get paid all year long, whether they work or not.

Because the pay is so poor, I must do other things. I must string together collections of adjunct course assignments from several different schools. I have taught six, seven, eight classes a semester at three or four different schools, and I know other adjuncts who have taught as many as ten or twelve. If I do that, I will hear snide remarks from department officials about my "romantic" gypsy existence, my nomad status, my freeway faculty life. I have worked other jobs and taught on the side. I have split my time between teaching four or five courses, a full-time load, and another job.

Being employed under these conditions makes it difficult, if not impossible, to do the things good teachers should do—regularly reevaluate and redesign my courses and lesson plans, be integrated into the issues, events and deadlines of the college, keep up on the current research in my field. Being employed under these conditions makes it difficult, if not impossible, to fully be the teacher the students are paying to have via their tuition dollars. I am usually off campus, unable to meet with them for conferences or extra help, uninvolved in and unaware of student activities and events. Hence, this makes me compliant in academia's system of double-barrelled fraud—fraud against the teacher; fraud against the student.

I am an adjunct. Although I am not treated as a professional, exemplary professionalism is constantly expected from me, far more than from any member of the full-time faculty. If I have poor course evaluations, I will be out. If I have a poor class observation, I will be out. If my students complain about me, legitimately or otherwise, I will be out. If a full-time faculty member faces any of this, he or she will be supported, worked with, helped. Full-time tenured faculty may not even be evaluated, and if their evaluations or course observations are poor, if their students complain about them, nothing affecting their employment or job security will be done.

I am an adjunct. Although I am expected to do a better job than full-time faculty, I am not included in department meetings. I have no input in department decisions. My opinion is rarely sought. In fact, in this paragon of academic freedom and open discourse in search of the truth, I know I will be punished if I honestly express my thoughts, and they are in conflict with those with power, particularly the anti-adjuncts with power. Oh yes, I am "welcome" to come to meetings, but usually they are scheduled during times I cannot come. If I do come, it must be on my own time and dime. Professional conferences, professional days, faculty forums all beckon with welcoming fingers, but I also must shoulder the cost if I find the time to attend. I would like to do them all, but I am usually unable to do any of them. My professional status quo, let alone my professional development, is something the schools will never sponsor, no matter how much they might gain from it. Even if I could do them all, I would feel like, and be treated like, the amateur pretending to be a "real" teacher.

I am an adjunct. Sometimes I must take money from my own pocket and spend it on the schools. Often, I must buy my own supplies, pay for photocopying, make long distance calls on my home phone to students. I know better than to even think of submitting a list of expenses to any school official for reimbursement. My home and car have turned into a jungle of papers and books because there is no place for me to keep things on campus. If I do not do these things, however, my teaching will suffer, my evaluations will show it, I will be out.

I understand that these incredible discrepancies in pay are based on both the required service and pedagogical "superiority" of the full-time faculty. I know they're supposed to do advising, committee work, department tasks. Many of them do their tasks very well, although that doesn't merit such discrepancy in pay. But I have known others, many others, who come in, teach their classes and leave, what adjuncts do. In fact, many full-time faculty are de-facto part-time, working other jobs on the side. Sometimes I have seen students wandering the halls, looking for the full-time professor who has an office, and office hours he or she is supposed to hold but is never there. I've heard many comments on how pleased they are over their 20-hour week, eight-month, $40,000 plus a year life.

I am an adjunct. I am an excellent teacher. I have given everything I could to my students despite the demeaning pay, the destructive working conditions and the lack of institutional support. I have watched the eyes of my former students light up with delighted recognition when I meet them, semesters later, in the parking lot. I've had students tell me that I am the best teacher they ever had. I've had students come up to me after class and say, "I never thought of it like that before." I've had students tell me how I inspire them, and teach them, and yet, I always respect them. I've had students in 101 classes ask me, again and again, "Are you teaching 102?" If I am, they seek my class out and sign up for it. I've had students take my classes on the advice of their friends who had me before, and I've had students join my class during add/drop because they're in a full-time teacher's class who they already know they cannot stand. My classes are not easy. I have high standards I hold them to. And I know I cannot get away with the things some full-time, tenured faculty pull without repercussion.

I am an adjunct; I have known insult and abuse. At a portfolio assessment session I attended, I watched a full-time faculty member take a handful of my students' essays to the program director and say, "These papers are too good to have come from an adjunct's class." At a department meeting I attended once, I presented a proposal for a course I wanted to develop. I wanted to show the department what a good full-time faculty person I would be, how active, how energetic, how creative. Instead, waves of hostility rolled at me from the full-time, tenured, comfortably complacent faculty. Here the adjunct was doing what none of them had even thought of doing in years; my course, completely without department support, went nowhere. At the end of the fall semester one year, a program director left a computer-generated Christmas card in the mailbox of all adjunct faculty. Taped to it were two Hershey chocolate kisses. The card and the kisses, she said, were our reward for our "talented teaching." Once, a department chair, a woman making close to $50,000 a year and complaining bitterly about having to come in during the summer to work on the schedule and not get extra pay for it, howled at me that I would be "OUT FOREVER!" if I insisted on a schedule change after SHE ignored, misread or misplaced my availability sheet and scheduled me for a class I could not do. I have been assigned classes the day before the beginning of the semester and have been expected to be as fully prepared on the first day of class as if I'd had days, or weeks, to get ready. I have been assigned classes full of difficult students and given no direction on how to handle them, no support in trying to handle them, but all the blame for whatever went wrong.

When there is one, I've gone to the union reps for help. I have never gotten help. I have gotten a lot of hand wringing, sympathetic clucking, clever smart remarks about the administrators, and promises that are never kept. One union rep, indicating the impotence and/or indifference of the union to the adjunct's fate, told me, "Leave the profession." Perhaps he doesn't realize that the power of the union is to a great extent measurable by how they are able to protect their weakest members. They are, however, quite adamant about collecting my dues.

I am an adjunct; I know about arrogance. In the process of watching college administrations rise and fall, I have seen college presidents dismiss the notion of raising the adjunct pay on the pretext that there is no money, or fight tooth and nail during collective bargaining agreements literally for years over giving us $100 more per course. But there is always money for what they want. One president told the board he wanted a million dollar salary and a job for life. Another president, clearly a man asleep on the job, expanded his "presidential suite" of offices until, like a cancer, they choked off the main hallway of the school. Those silly pests, the students, had to go upstairs or down to get to one side of the school from the other. (And they wonder why their retention rate is so low.) I have seen presidents, who after wailing at the fiscal impossibility of giving the adjuncts a raise, turn around and give himself and all the administrators ten thousand dollar raises. I have watched administrators protest at making the working conditions better for adjuncts while misappropriating funds up to the point of being exposed and fired.

This arrogant incompetence (or vice versa) infuriates me. No one signs up for one of my classes because of the presidents. No one encourages a friend to take my class because of the deans. But the academic sideshow must go on. I stand in filthy classrooms, where there is no chalk or heat, where a broken clock looks down on us through a cracked face, and do the best I can. Students, dreaming fools or cynical pragmatics, hunch in tiny, dilapidated desks between minimum wage jobs and post graduate debt and believe this will make life better. If we want a taste of luxury, all we have to do is drop by the administration building.

I am an adjunct; I know hypocrisy. I am often surrounded by liberal men and women who cluck and coo about the plights of "women, people of color, gays and lesbians, the old, the poor, the ill, the third world, and the working classes" with all the politically correct/plastic emotionalism academe has given its stamp of approval to. In the process, they either ignore, endorse or propagate the injustices done to the underclass of faculty that surrounds and outnumbers them. And there are times when sexism, racism, homophobia, ageism are quite okay—when directed against an adjunct. Perhaps they have failed to realize that equal pay for equal work should be a tenet of any consistent liberal philosophy. Perhaps they have been able to dismiss inherent liberal concepts like the right of all people to earn a decent living wage. In fact, academe itself, the bastion of liberalism, according to supporters and critics alike, turns cold, cruel and despotic over its own underclass. I have watched former adjunct faculty, who could at the time, complain loudly and bitterly, justifiably so, over the way they were treated, turn 180 degrees around when for some reason or another, they land a full-time job. Academe has canonized that great Shirley Jackson story, "The Lottery," but many of its members evidently still don't get the message of the rock-throwing parable. It isn't wrong anymore when it's done to someone else.

I am an adjunct; I am ambitious. I have done this, put up with this, with the hope of getting a full time job. Maybe I want the job because I want to be paid and treated better for doing the work I love. Maybe I want it because I want to see how good a job I can do when all I have to do is teach four or five classes a semester, advise students, attend meetings and be on committees. Maybe I want it because I want to be treated with the respect the other class of faculty who do the same work as me receive. And maybe I just want it because I want a twenty-hour a week, eight month, $40,000 a year job for life too.

I have been interviewed for full-time positions at all the schools I've worked and been passed up every time. For years, one school promised me a full-time position as soon as "they" let us hire anyone. When "they" finally did, a new anti-adjunct president was firmly entrenched in power. He insisted on a "national search for quality minority" candidates; he hired five white outsiders. At another school, a jury-of-one dean interviewed all the adjuncts who applied and then turned around and hired an outsider, one of her personal friends. During my interview, I saw her stifling yawns and looking at her watch. She willingly wasted taxpayers' money and my time and played with my emotions, but she wasn't at all interested in what I had to say; her mind was already made up. At another school, I was passed up for a job because I was told I was "out of touch" with the needs of the

7

school, although I can't imagine how the outsiders hired could be considered to be more "in touch" from a cover letter, a resume and one or two interviews. It was, of course, the perfect cover for a string of petty, hateful resentments espoused by a pseudo-liberal dean that had nothing to do with my teaching or my ability to be an effective member of the department.

Yet all of these schools continued to let me teach their classes. Representatives from all three have continued to praise my work and, when asked, have written me glowing letters of recommendation for other jobs. Administrators of all three have identified me as a valuable member of the faculty. It makes no sense. It's reasoning that wouldn't fly in Critical Thinking 100, Logic 101 and Ethics 102 (all taught, no doubt, by adjuncts). If I'm good enough to teach here, why am I not good enough to be full time? If I'm not good enough to be full-time, why are they letting me teach here at all? What can any outsider say in an hour-long interview that overrides years of a solid work record, a paper trail of course evaluations, a history of knowing the person and their work? What is it other than innate, institutional anti-adjunct bias?

I am an adjunct; I know there is more to this than me. I know schools all over the country are strapped for funds. I know that government and public support for higher education is inconsistent if not altogether missing. I know about the approach/avoidance attitude about education in this society. Corporate America decrees we be degreed, but the government, the military, the business world and the church really don't want educated, thinking people. The colleges are caught between the whims of their benefactors and their own survival; true education is rendered impotent. I know that even most full-time faculty are grossly underpaid for the work that so many swear is so important, as most people working in human services in this society are. I know that caught between velvet job security and the cactus values of the larger culture, it has caused many full-time faculty to turn cynical, complacent and abusive of the system. I know that terms like "competitive" and "supply and demand" and "buyer's market" are all tossed about to justify whatever someone wants to justify. I even understand that it is necessary to use part-time help. But I don't understand the abuse. The insistence on setting terms that are unfair and exploitative and then blaming us for accepting them. If we must have low pay, why not more job security? If we must have no job security, why not better pay? If we must have low pay and no job security, then why must we also face the exploitation, the abuse, the malice and the insults? I can't imagine why they haven't figured it out yet. Can college officials expect the outside world to support and honor their institutions when, from the inside, a huge group of *teachers* are treated so poorly? Aren't they really saying something about the value of teachers? The value of teaching? The value of students? The value of their own institutions?

I am an adjunct; I am to be pitied. I bought the bag of lies we call the American Dream. I was intoxicated on the Nitrous Oxide idealism forced upon me in graduate school. I believed caring, working hard, doing a good job mattered and would add up to something concrete. Instead, I find myself on a wheel that turns but goes nowhere. I don't expect this situation to change. I know I have joined the huge group of teachers who become permanent adjuncts, who do a good job only to get one more chance to do it again. I know I do not have it in me to become the asshole or the ass-kisser I will need to become in order to get an administrator to give me a full-time job.

I have watched my self-esteem drop, drop, drop from doing work that is, theoretically, enhancing the self-esteem of my students. I have seen the tired eyes, the worn clothes, the ancient cars of long-term adjuncts. I have looked into their eyes as they have failed to look back into mine. I have heard other adjunct laments. "I feel like a ghost here," one woman told me in the hall one day. "I feel like such a failure," another woman told me. "I tell them this work is important, that it leads to success, but look at me." I have known thirty year old men living at home with their parents, forty year old women teaching college and going hungry, uninsured fifty year olds with serious illnesses. I have known adjunct teachers who hand out As and Bs like vitamins and help students cheat on their exams so they'll get good course evaluations. I've watched people fall into obsessive relationships with their idealism and their pedagogy because it is the one defense against despair.

I know it is a fate I do not want.

I will leave the profession. I will go back to school (Ha! Ha!). I will get another degree, or a new one. I will start a business. I will find a boring nine-to-five and push papers for better pay and treatment. But teaching, even at its worse, is very seductive. Anyone who's ever gone into it, or gotten out of it, knows that. So maybe I'll just do it one more semester, one more year. Because I love the work. I love my field. I love my students. I love the energy of the classroom and those special moments when I can do something good, when I see their eyes glowing and their faces shining, knowing that I am reaching them, I am doing something worthwhile.

I am a dreamer. I am an idealist. I am a victim. I am a whore. I am a fool.

I am an adjunct.

Adjuncts Are Not People

by Kate Gale

My friend from back East called me up the other day. We got to chatting about this and that; it was snowing in New Hampshire in February, and I claimed to be jogging, getting a tan and planting out cucumbers, same old, same old. So she asked me, do I have Lo-Jack. She's heard it's this security system for protecting your car that everybody in Los Angeles has to have because we need to protect our cars from being stolen, and then, I got to laughing. I mean, I really broke down. And I couldn't fake any more that I'm living the high life out here in the freaking, sunny, palm tree lined streets of Los Angles.

You see, I'm a freeway flyer. An adjunct English instructor. I teach at least ten classes a semester at six different colleges and universities. And I barely make a living, so I don't have Lo-Jack; nothing like it. What I have, I told my friend, is a car with 180,000 miles on it. It's not even six years old. As soon as it was paid for, I called my insurance company, who is charging me $1,100 every six months to insure my car, which is currently worth about $500, to take off the comp and collision. She asked me if I have Lo-Jack. She doesn't know I lie awake at night, dreaming someone will steal my piece of crap car, and they will steal it in the evening. I leave the gate open, and the keys in the car on purpose. They will steal it in the evening so it won't overheat and break down before they make it to Tijuana to sell my car, and then maybe I can get another piece of crap in which I will spend most of my waking hours as I drive from one college to the next.

I have nightmares that I drive to the wrong college, the wrong university, that I get up and say the wrong thing, although this has never happened. The car is where I spend my life, speeding from one class to another, and it is barely running, I told my friend. Nobody I know has a security system on his or her car. We are the lowest form of life. We crawl the belly of existence in our crappy Volkswagens and our small Japanese automobiles with so much mileage, the odometer looks like the wheel of fortune whipping in the wind. We grip the wheels of our spinning tin cans. We pray we get there on time.

Sometimes I think the worst thing about being a freeway flyer isn't the driving; it's the constant bouts with illness. At twenty-five when I started this, I had never had medical insurance, never been hospitalized, never had antibiotics for any reason. Now I am on antibiotics fully one third of the time. I go from one illness to another—kidney infections, strep, bronchitis, pneumonia, mono. One semester, after a long series of illnesses, I had continued to teach. I finally collapsed and had to be hospitalized. I woke up to find that the antibiotics that I am constantly taking were finally being given to me intravenously, dripping into my veins, making me feel like I was on a barge of hallucinations. I could see the faces of students crowding around my bedside. I held out my hands. "Go away," I said. "I'll be back," and I passed out again. I woke up in the middle of the night, saw the number above the door and wrote a poem called "Room 901."

I remembered I had a job interview at an LA college in three days. I had to get better. Three days later, I asked my doctor to release me, and she consented at eight-thirty in the morning. I still hadn't kept any food down, hadn't walked further than a few steps. My boyfriend took the day off work and came to pick me up. The interview was in one hour, and it was a forty-five minute drive to get there. He brought my clothes. I couldn't drive, but I could dress. He hadn't brought socks or nylons, just heels and a suit. No make-up, but I was in no position to complain. I pulled the suit over my bones and stood up. He'd brought lipstick, and I put it on. I looked pale, awkward, angular, my face a white slab with that slash of glittering mauve across it. He drove; I rested. I walked on his arm to the elevator, went up by myself. The interview required a teaching demonstration. Somehow for twenty minutes, I stood, talked, then sat down, answered questions. At the bottom of the elevator, he caught me and carried me back to the car. Of course, as I found out later, they never even had considered hiring me. They had already decided to give the job to someone else. But I had to try. A full-time job would mean making twice as much money for half the teaching, and how long can I go on like this? I don't know.

Sometimes I think the only thing that keeps me going in life, besides the love of my children and boyfriend, is my writing. I write poetry and novels, but that doesn't help when it comes to getting jobs. It isn't even noticed. No matter how much you write (I've written five books, three of which have been published), if you are an adjunct, nobody notices. Full-time teachers don't see you as fully human, so they don't ask how your writing is. They don't see you at all.

At one college, I share office space one day a week with one of the full-time instructors. He put a sign with my name by the door as a sort of welcoming gesture. The next week, the secretary of the English Department wrote me a note. Two of the full-time teachers were in a fury at the arrogance of my putting up a nameplate. The two instructors she mentioned weren't even people I knew. That's when I first realized that the full-time people wanted us to stay invisible, their own private, unseen labor force. Which is why the hope adjuncts start off with, that they will eventually get a full-time job, is thoroughly gone by their second year. At this college, where I have been teaching for eight years, they don't even interview their own adjuncts. They have adjuncts who have been there longer than me, for ten years. They don't even deign to interview them. They hire people from outside.

Each college has its own way of humiliating you, of letting you know that you are a second class citizen. At one college, the full-time people can have their paychecks automatically deposited; the part-time people can not. At another college, the full-time people can use their writings, articles, and readings as a flex activity, while the part-time people have to go to a particularly boring yearly meeting at the college, which is all adjunct people wishing to go home, sitting around, staring at their hands in an auditorium. The previously mentioned college, where they won't interview adjuncts, is surely the kindest to us. It is one of the few colleges where adjuncts are allowed to teach creative writing classes. Most colleges have adjuncts teaching all Freshman composition and developmental English. Even so, since I've been there, I've never heard of an adjunct being interviewed.

I see adjuncts as being a permanent slave class at the colleges. I see that full-time faculty have no interest in ever having to treat us as human beings. The ideal would be that anyone who gets hired as an adjunct and receives positive reviews would automatically become a tenure track instructor in four years. But *They*, the ones with offices, would have to vote for that, and *They* never will, anymore than the wealthy in this country will vote to share their wealth with the lower classes.

What I think about as I pull into my little driveway in my beat up car, driving back from picking up yet another prescription of penicillin, is how much Jésus (pronounced Hay-soos) and I have in common, and yet, I think about his life and feel I have little to complain about. Jésus is a landscape gardener for most of the people in my neighborhood. He does all the gardening and most of the people don't ever speak to him, don't even really see him at all.

One day, I drove up, and I saw a man next door talking to a landscape architect about what to do to improve his lawn. Jésus and his brother were leaning on their old truck while this white landscape gardener was getting paid $50 an hour to advise my neighbor.

"Why don't you ask Jésus?" I asked, and he laughed like that's a good joke.

"Jésus does the dirty work; Raymond does the planning." But I've talked to Raymond. He knows less about gardening than Jésus because Jésus does gardening everywhere, every day. "Anyway, Jésus and I don't even speak the same language." I turned away, thinking of the gaps between the haves and the have-nots, growing wider every day.

Later, Jésus and I sat on the lawn drinking lemonade. He tried my boyfriend's salsa and told me that, for a gringo, this was excellent salsa, and we laughed. I asked what he thinks about Raymond, and Jésus shrugged. He told me that he likes to work in the grass, he likes the feel of the soil, and I know what he means. When you are actually doing your job, when you're in the classroom, it's good, working with the students.

I remember when my thirteen year-old-stepson came to work with me and said that he would like to be an adjunct, and how I felt sick thinking of it. "What would you do if your son wanted to do this work?" I asked Jésus. He shook his head. "Not going to happen, not to my son. Never, I won't allow it," and that's how I feel too, not my lovely Nicholas. I can't let this happen to him.

But Jésus loves the soil, the grass, the flowers. "Most people don't even see the sky any more," he told me. "I do." And again, I know, I still see my students, and I read their papers, and I like them. "Of course, I don't speak English and most of the people I work for don't speak Spanish," Jésus told me, "but they don't see me at all." And again, I know what he means; when I walk through the hallways of *Them* who have offices, I feel invisible. I don't think they have a clue about my life or what I do. We're not colleagues anymore than Jésus and Raymond are colleagues. We don't speak the same language. Mine is the language of clay; theirs the language of marble.

In the end, you don't really exist. Walk by the offices. Real teachers have their own office. You don't have one. You don't exist. You aren't anywhere. Jésus tells me nothing will ever change, but sometimes that's good, he says; do you hear the grass growing?

No Exit
or My Life as a Gypsy on the Part-Time Circuit

by Jim Neal

For as long as I can remember, I have loved all aspects of English, from grammar to literature, and by tenth grade, I had decided I wanted to be a writer. I attended graduate school, determined to model my career after Henry Crews, who teaches at a junior college in Gainsville, Florida, and writes articles, short stories and novels on the side. As I was finishing my class work in the spring of 1980, the department head called me aside and said, "Jim I have some good news and some bad news. The good news is that due to a number of factors, people are fleeing education, especially the humanities, like rats from the proverbial sinking ship. Those who hold the remaining jobs will be retiring around 1990, creating a 'Great Teacher Shortage,' which means that even if you never earn a Ph.D., you'll be able to teach at a major university, and perhaps even head a department."

"What could possibly be the bad news?" I asked in all innocence.

"You'll have to live until then," was his reply.

I spent the next four years giving tours, driving a truck, tending bar and dispatching freight. In March of 1984, I found employment at a proprietary school, where I taught all the English courses and most of the general studies courses. For the remainder of the decade, I was paid an average of $16,000 to teach twenty to twenty-four classes per year, was treated like a clerk and was frequently pressured to bend academic, ethical and legal standards.

Throughout this period, I was sustained by the knowledge that in 1990, I would leave the proprietary field and find a position in the publicly funded sector, where I would earn enough money and have sufficient disposable time to start on a doctorate and resume my writing. In March of 1990, I tendered my resignation and was delighted when I was offered classes at a university and a community college. You can imagine how my hope quickly turned to dismay as I discovered I would have to put in nearly as many hours and had the potential of earning what I had at the proprietary schools. I was told by a kindly but misinformed woman that a part-time assignment was only a training period, and I would be awarded a full-time position after a couple of years if things worked out. However, some of my co-workers at the university had been on the part-time circuit for ten years and longer and had yet to be offered a full-time position. Since then, I have applied for over one hundred positions and have yet to be invited for an interview. Furthermore, I found that there was no assurance that I would have a position by the end of the term. One department head told me, "Without a Ph.D., I won't hire you. With a Ph.D., I probably won't hire you."

Since then, I have taught at a half dozen schools. Each time I move, I must learn a new curriculum, a new text, new assignments, new scheduling (everything from self-paced to weekend, every other weekend, eight-week, nine-week, quarter, trimester and semester, each of which requires a different approach) and a new pedagogy. All employers insist they want "high academic standards," which I have found can mean anything from actual high academic standards, to indoctrination in Marxist/Feminist/revisionism, to patting the students on the back and giving them A's, regardless of their academic performance. If I am not sufficiently intuitive, I'm not asked back. I am especially uncomfortable at institutions where tuition is high and enrollment is low. I know that students are very hard to come by, and part-time English teachers are a dime a dozen. The students are quick to sense that they are much more important to the school than I am. They know that a complaint or bad evaluation can put an end to my presence at their institution, and I find it difficult to teach students who know they have my economic and professional future in their hands.

Thrice a year, I send my resume to every school within a one hundred mile radius of Kansas City. I go begging, and until I'm assigned enough classes for the next term, I live in fear of losing my $39,000 house and all I have worked for. Last year, one of my fellow part-timers took her own life. I'm sure that the stress and anxiety associated with the part-time circuit was a major factor in her tragedy.

Let me say that the term "part-time" is a misnomer. I have met many people in my years of teaching who are euphemistically called "adjunct." Of those, I can count on one hand, with fingers to spare, the lucky few for whom teaching is actually a part-time proposition—a hobby which stimulates the mind, occupies otherwise idle hours and supplements the breadwinner's already sufficient income.

If my thrice-a-year mailing is successful, the rewards generally consist of a roster, a text, a room full of students and a check in the mail. I feel like the occasional stray dog that wanders into my neighborhood. In the few days that pass before the animal control takes it away to euthanasia or a research lab, compassionate neighbors will set out bowls of food and lament the poor dog's fate, but they don't invite it inside, name it or pet it.

I teach six to eight classes per semester, and I take all the summer work I can. I spend an average of eight hours driving an average of four hundred miles per week. This earns me $16,000 to $18,000 per year. Over the span of my teaching "career," in spite of all my wife has done, in spite of going without most luxuries and a few of what many would consider necessities, we have slid an additional $1,000 per year deeper into debt, and I can therefore sympathize with the farmer who, when asked what he was going to do with the million dollars he had won in the lottery, replied, "I'm gonna keep on farmin' till this runs out."

Since I earn so little per class, I must teach more than I should. Since I teach so many classes, I don't have time to help around the house, but since I earn so little, I must do things which most people hire others to do. I have no automatic dishwasher, so I do my dishes by hand. My kids can't understand why they can't send out for pizza as their friends do. I can't afford to send out for pizza, so I make one from scratch. Since I earn so little, my wife must work all the overtime she can, which is considerable, leaving me all the shopping, cooking, dishes, vacuuming and ironing. I do the maintenance on my cars, take care of our two children and run them to their various destinations. Trying to keep up with my obligations in the home and teach one and a half to a double full-time load leaves me little time for sleep, and the opportunity for personal or professional growth is nil.

People sometimes say, "But you love teaching." I do. I love teaching. My life has been a testament to that. I also love peach pie, but I wouldn't care to eat it four times per day, seven days per week, fifty-two weeks per year. And I believe that even the most ferociously optimistic person, which I am not, would experience difficulty in maintaining a cheerful demeanor in a system in which his best and most conscientious efforts will yield, at best, one more limited opportunity to do his utmost, whereas anything less could end his career.

I must confess I feel nothing like I thought I would feel at forty-six. Each day I realize the extent to which vitality is deserting me. I am no longer young, but though I am not yet old, I am tired. I don't know how much longer I will be equal to the demands placed upon me. I have health insurance, thanks to my wife, but I have no pension, nor any hope of ever having one. There is no way I will be able to contribute financially to my children's college education. Indeed, at this time it seems unlikely that they will be able to participate in the system that I've spent my life promoting. When I contemplate my future, I am overwhelmed with a profound dread. If I may say so, life on the part-time circuit sucks.

However, allow me to ruminate briefly on what little good I can say about the situation.

First, I do not believe the part-time system is a nefarious plot—the demonic brainchild of some morally bankrupt MBA's diseased and overwrought imagination. It is simply supply and demand. Were I of a paranoid bent, I could possibly suspect that the tabled and much touted "Great Teacher Shortage" was nothing more than a ploy to dupe more unsuspecting fools into the field and assure the prolongation of what is, in fact, a "Great Teacher Glut," thereby keeping wages low, as dispossessed farmers were lured to California with promises of good-paying jobs during the Great Depression. But I don't believe that.

Also I suspect the system is as onerous to administrators as it is to those of us who labor in it. Just as I must go a-begging three times per year, my employers must select from a parade of pathetic hopefuls enough warm, degreed bodies to staff their classes. Surely this is a poor utilization of their time and energies. And just as I have no idea what is expected of me in each new environment, my employers have no guarantee that what appeared to be a sound candidate during the interview might not at midterm, with warning, suddenly transmogrify into a raving pederast.

Third, some employers assign us our classes in a timely manner and sometimes even go out of their way to give us a schedule that is convenient for us. I cannot express how much that is appreciated.

Fourth, we meet many wonderful people. I don't just mean the students, faculty and staff. I especially mean the other adjuncts, who often offer academic advice and emotional support to one another.

Fifth, my experience on the part-time circuit has been an education in itself. My exposure to the different texts, pedagogies and environments has broadened my perspective immeasurably. In addition, I've had the opportunity to teach an incredible variety of classes. It is not much of an exaggeration to say that if I ever have an opportunity to start on a Ph.D. program, I will be hard pressed to find courses I haven't already taught.

Sixth, I've become one hell of a cook.

But my years as an adjunct have obliterated any trace of egotism and pride, not to mention confidence, I might once have had.

A Week in the Life
of a Part-Time Teacher

by Diana Claitor

Eva left me a note and a little gift that I found when I returned for the summer session. Eva is a Salvadoran, a
mother of two who had been studying in the tutoring lab
every day for months, struggling though the Comp I obstacle
course. The card read: "Diana, thank you for so much help. I got
the B!"

The other mail in my box was not nearly that pleasant —
mostly memos about new titles, computer foul-ups and the general chaos created by the reorganization of the college. Worst of
all, the department heads had been summarily fired, and there
was nobody to go to with the unexpected questions that come at
the beginning of each semester. What to do with the Chinese
student who has a degree in engineering but who only speaks
about 25 words of English? Who has the departmental entrance
exam for our developmental writing classes? Where can I hide

from the overly talkative paranoid schizophrenic who tells me she's been banned from all the other campuses but is now back on her meds?

At the same time, it turned out the tutoring labs were being placed under new departments. The labs, the mainstay for most of us who teach developmental classes, were in an uproar, and my lab already made one small but significant change: the file cabinet with folders for each instructor was being removed. Those files were the one reliable place we could leave tests or information for students. Since we adjuncts have variable hours and no separate offices of our own, whenever students missed a class, this was the place they could pick up materials. (And it got students into the lab, where they might actually get some help.)

The disappearance of the file cabinet seemed symbolic – one of the many ways part-timers were being cut loose.

Both of my classes had very low enrollment. I explained to the first group that we'd probably be canceled, and one student followed me out to my car with tears in her eyes.

"I've planned this for three years," she said. "I work nights. I got a deal worked out with Financial Aid. I got everything balanced just right, so I can go to school and do a good job but keep my job. This class is required, and I GOT to have it at this time of day."

I told her I'd carry her message to whatever higher authority I could find – and I did have some small hope since the college was supposed to give special consideration to these state-mandated courses without which many students are bounced out of school. In the meantime, I discovered that our departing department head had hired two new adjuncts to teach fall classes even though there weren't enough classes to sustain the instructors already here. I suppose that was her little way of saying "thanks" to the veteran teachers who'd put in years here.

It was storming at the first meeting of my other class, and shortly after I gave them the entrance exam, we were evacuated to a room on the ground floor. A tornado was ripping through a subdivision to the west of us. The entire population of the campus spent forty nervous minutes crammed together. When my students returned to our room, another class was sitting there. The room was double booked. The other teacher acted like an ass; I took my class to an empty room down the hall and finished the test there.

The next day I found a phone message from a student I'd tutored many times. Julia is an African American woman with three children and a huge smile. Two semesters ago, I supported her in a disagreement with an English professor over a grade. She had struggled hard to make the grades necessary to get into a nursing program, but one hurdle remained: an assessment test. Julia was understandably nervous and wanted me to tutor her one last time. I told her the hours I'd be available in the lab.

Despite evidence of the students' need for my particular classes, the college canceled both sections. Of course, if affected me as well: now my only income for the summer would be the tutoring along with any freelance journalism and research I could scare up. Since the administration cut the lab's budget, I probably wouldn't be able to work as many hours in the lab either.

That night, while drinking too much wine, I came to realize that no matter how much I loved teaching and tutoring here, my time at the college was coming to an end.

During the next week, I came in early and met with the division head (whose job had been eliminated but whose duties went on), and we tried to find ways for the nine students in my canceled classes to stay in school. Each one had a complicated schedule, and there were very few classes to offer them as an alternative to mine. I called the students, called the division head at home, and even made a special trip to another campus to fill out a special form so one student could jump a level and get a writing class at the right time at another campus. The division head thanked me for my efforts.

I ran into a student – a refrigerator-sized ex-football player with the face of a plump girl – whom I taught last semester. He said, "Hey, Miz Claitor, I'm going to take that next writing class in the fall. When are you teaching it?" I told him I wouldn't be teaching here in the fall. His sweet face fell. He asked, "Why?" I couldn't think how to sum up all the complicated reasons, and I didn't want him to lose confidence in the college, so I just said they couldn't offer me enough classes and wished him luck.

Julia showed up for the big finale tutoring session. Her little boy was with her because the two older kids couldn't keep him today; I wondered if she'd be able to concentrate. He had some crayons, and I got him a pile of used computer paper. Julia and I discussed the best way to "psyche yourself" for a test. I gave her a grammar pre-test, and later I saw that she was doing so well she could stop, but she wanted to do the whole thing. Beaming at me, she blurted, "Diana, I just LOVE learning."

Trying for matter-of-fact, I nodded and told her I felt exactly the same way. Then I went away so she could finish; when I returned, she said, "I think this is exactly what I needed to get ready. I knew you would know what I should work on." I told her to pat herself on the back – she's the one who's taught herself.

The following week, I went for my first interview for a "real job," meaning work with benefits and some degree of security and support. But to my mind, this use of the word "real" renders it meaningless. Teaching in a community college is as real as it gets – our students are real people with real needs, students who need committed teachers. It seems, however, that the teacher is no longer considered essential or deserving of respect. To those in power who somehow, against all logic, consider themselves educators – to those people, I was just not real.

Dispatches from the Adjunct Universe

by R. Piehler

There isn't much certainty in an adjunct instructor's life. You never know what classes you'll be teaching from one semester to the next or, in extreme cases, even where you'll be teaching. You are on the bottom of the food chain when it comes to schedule-planning, and even if you are assigned a class, there's no guarantee that the class won't be canceled at the last second because of low enrollment, or that someone higher in the predatory cycle won't snatch one of your classes away should one of theirs be canceled. (This practice is actually allowed by the union-sanctioned contract at the college where I teach.) Your classroom is not really "yours" and neither is your shared office space. You travel, insofar as it is possible, with a portable teaching apparatus of notes, slides, books, handouts, whatever. You and your bulging bag cross rivers and traverse whole boroughs. You wonder if you are teaching enough classes--will there be money to get through the summer? You wonder if you are teaching too many--how will you have time to work on your dissertation? You wonder if the photocopier will be in working order when you arrive for your evening class, or if you will have to trudge down the block in the freezing sleet to the copy shop where you will pay for the evening's handouts with your own money.

Some of your students will instantly lose the handouts anyway, despite your warnings that you don't have extra copies. Some of your students have worked all day at difficult and/or paralyzingly boring jobs and cannot stay awake in your class, especially when you turn down the lights and fire up the slide projectors. They sag, doze, on a few occasions even snore or drool at the back of the room. Sometimes you wake them during the class break and suggest coffee or a splash of cold water, and they sheepishly agree, but they are not embarrassed, certainly not mortified. They want credit for showing up, for not missing class altogether, as though listening, taking notes, participating and reacting were somehow optional. You used to take it personally when someone in your class showed such uncloaked disinterest, and you spent long subway or car rides home feeling demoralized and shockingly peripheral, and you would try, try, try to make the Italian Renaissance or Dutch Baroque painting more palatable and applicable to your students' lives. You'd try to point out the universality of certain themes, how Giotto's *Lamentation* was not just an important stylistic turning point in the history of painting but in fact a wondrous and touching depiction of the grief that any parent would feel for a dead child. You think it works sometimes, but you're not sure: are the nodding heads agreeing with you, or are your students once again on the verge of passing out in your overheated classroom?

During the evening class, clock-watching is rampant after the break (for those who actually return after the break; there is minor but still visible attrition) and it becomes something even more palpable as 9 PM approaches: impatience. You've learned to read the signs: there's a certain hunched pose, the polar opposite of the early evening slouch, which signals an attention-span shutdown. The hunch spreads like mold over the classroom by 8:45, and if it still seems a polite and possibly ambiguous physical manifestation of boredom, what follows is not: notebooks closed, train schedules unfolded and consulted, multiple

27

sweatshirts and coats wrapped once more around bodies. You're still talking, but no one listens. One woman clutches a cell-phone during the final quarter-hour, week after week. You've forbidden them in the classroom, directed your students on the very first day of class and in the strongly worded syllabus to turn off phones, beepers, pagers, etc. This woman cannot wait for you to wrap up the evening's lecture. You're convinced she's heard nothing of your final fifteen minutes for the entire semester. She wants out.

And, tiredly, so do you. You've arranged your lecture to end at a logical juncture. Open parentheses have no place in an evening class that meets just once a week. By next Monday, only the most alert of your students will be able to tell you where you left off. You ask this question at the beginning of every class—"What did we finish with last week?"—and a vast silence blankets the classroom until someone flips the pages of their notebook and timidly offers, "Umm, Moses?" Yes, it's Moses. You dim the lights and project a slide of Michelangelo's *Moses* onto the screen, hoping that someone will remember and react to the sheer physicality of the sculpture, if nothing else. You've tried to contemporize Moses for them, a strategy you resort to more and more each semester—do you all see Moses' biceps, doesn't he look like he works out at some Old Testament gym at least five times a week?—and again some of your students nod. But what if you've gone too far? What if when you show the same slide two weeks from now during the midterm exam, all you get back inscribed in thirty bluebooks is that Moses went to the gym?

There are a lot of what-if questions asked on cold Monday nights in the cold adjunct universe. What if you'd gone to law school or business school like your parents hoped is a frequent one, so frequent that it's become an in-joke among your adjunct brethren. Other what-ifs are nothing more than rephrased complaints: what if all your students actually spoke and could express themselves in decent English, what if they didn't just download big chunks of predigested information from the Internet whenever you assigned them a paper, what if you could go back in time and correct their entire defective pre-college educations in a single blinding flash and transform them into young men and women who want to learn simply for the sake of learning, which you are not yet too old and too resigned and too beaten down to remember as a crucial part of your own undergraduate experience?

What if, at this very late date, you changed your major and your goals and your economic expectations (laughable as they are) and your career path and said "No thanks" when next semester's schedule is passed around, and you bequeathed your battered steel desk and dusty lamp to someone younger and more immediately needy?

You won't, of course. The rewards of teaching may be intermittent and transparent, but they are there, lurking in the ether of the classroom. It only takes one serious inquiry, one student who genuinely wants to know why a certain painting looks the way it does, one student who asks for some reading suggestions beyond the assigned textbook (your reaction: shock and disbelief, but the most pleasant kind), one student who shows up during your office hours not to plead implausibly about missing an exam but just to talk about art. It can be an evening when, yawns and dozing notwithstanding, you connect with the slides on the screen and channel your enthusiasm (and maybe your personal experience of standing in front of that painting or sculpture or cathedral), and there is a single pair of shining eyes in your dim classroom that cancels out all the dulled ones.

You're nothing if not pragmatic, and you realize that such rewards are ephemeral and quickly exhausted. It is hard not to feel that the part-time teaching universe is also a vacant one, that the opportunities to move up in the department don't exist, that your colleagues are burnt out, that the full-timers ("lifers," you like to call them) are probably worse. And yet: those brief flares in your teaching week are a kind of fuel. They are enough to sustain you from class to class, and they keep you hovering at low altitude above a mucky, sticky lagoon of apathy. (You can see some of the full-timers' hands twitching weakly in the muck if you look down, by the way.) These flares of communication and connection are also, in the end, the only things in the adjunct universe you really own.

My Worst Adjunct Horror Stories

by Edward Tassinari

I taught my first college level course as an adjunct instructor in 1977--over twenty years and at four institutions, two in Florida and two in New York. In 1982, I was awarded a Ph.D. in Inter-American studies from the Graduate School of International Studies at the University of Miami. In all that time, I never once obtained an interview for a tenure track college position.

Everyone in academia knows that employing adjunct instructors at a fraction of the income of tenure track professors is higher education's dirty little secret. For years, I maintained a file of articles and letters, clipped primarily from *The Chronicle of Higher Education* with evidence to that end.

My worst fear in regard to adjunct teaching jobs was getting the last minute offer you want to refuse but can't. Saying no is akin to the substitute teacher refusing too many early morning phone calls from personnel secretaries on frozen January mornings. You're damned if you do, and damned if you don't. I traveled that road for a while also. To adequately prepare a college level course requires several months of reading, note-taking, writing lectures, making course outlines, crafting the syllabus, etc. As an adjunct, one doesn't always have the luxury of time to organize a course in that fashion.

I landed my first adjunct position on a Thursday evening, four days before the start of the semester. I was assigned to teach Social Sciences 102 to a class of medical care providers working towards an undergraduate degree at the medical center branch of a Florida community college. Halfway through the semester, I threw out the badly written textbook assigned to me by the department (the book was a watered down mishmash of countless disciplines; it was simplistic, overly politicized and poorly suited, even for a high school civics class), and we began to discuss contemporary national and international issues. My students and I both struggled, but in the end, we survived and learned from each other.

After that semester, I explained to the administrators that I needed to spend more time working on my dissertation, but that I wanted to teach again the next fall. I was promised employment and spent part of the following summer putting course material together, only to learn a few days before the semester was to begin that there had been some misunderstanding. I had been misinformed. There were no openings for adjuncts at that time.

A few days later, I registered for graduate research credits in my graduate program. When I returned from registration, the woman, in whose home I rented a room, told me she had taken a call for me from the school. At the last minute, they were looking for someone to teach an adjunct course as another instructor had pulled out. When I couldn't be reached, somebody else got the job. By the time I called back, it was too late.

The best was yet to come. A few weeks later, I received a paycheck, ostensibly payment for the course I had hoped to teach but wasn't. How my name landed at the top of the class roll, God only knows. I was seriously tempted to cash the check and whatever others that might have followed, but although we adjuncts may be masochists at heart, we are honorable men and women. I called the personnel department, told them of their mistake and returned the check. I never heard from them again.

A few years later, after working as a teaching assistant, research assistant and a stint with a consulting firm composed of graduate students with an expertise in Latin America, I landed another adjunct job four days before the start of the semester. The course was interesting and within my area of specialization, and the students were bright and reasonably motivated. No horror stories there, although I spent the better part of fourteen weeks writing lectures (not much time or space for student centered focus) and putting together readings when the textbook utilized for the first half of the course was out of stock for the second half. I lost fifteen pounds from nervous tension required to prepare on the fly. A month after the semester ended, I left Florida for good and returned to my family's home in a suburb of New York City. A few months after that, an adjunct position opened up in my field at the university in Florida. I wasn't there to compete for it.

My most recent experience as an adjunct was by far the longest at any institution. Roughly six years (twelve semesters) between 1986 and 1994, teaching history at a state college in the Bronx. Starting as a per diem substitute lecturer, I progressed to half time, then to full time teaching, as an adjunct assistant professor of history. There was even an ever-so-faint hint of something more permanent in the way of employment. Then came the fatal week in late November 1990 when a suddenly discovered state budgetary shortfall (conveniently unearthed after the gubernatorial election) made seven professors at the college expendable for the spring semester (not all were adjuncts). I was among that number.

Within the space of a week, I had progressed from preparing to teach a full-time load the following semester to teaching a half-time load to not teaching at all. According to the terms of my contract (a rather standard, two page "appointment letter" normally tendered to adjuncts), I could not be terminated with less than forty-five days before the following semester was to begin. I was given notice with about a week to spare. Having taught for more than six consecutive semesters at the college, I had achieved a certain classification as an adjunct, according to the union contract we worked under, which should have protected me from such a termination. Yet when I re-read my employment letter, that vital designation was omitted. Accident or design?

As my department chairperson told me when I departed at the end of the semester, "No one else will thank you for your efforts on our behalf, so let me be the person to do so." I appreciated that. Subsequently, a group of students, primarily freshmen, began a petition campaign to register their protest at the firing of the seven. I don't know all the details, but apparently a combination of higher authorities and upper classmen squelched that effort. The academic union to which I then belonged did nothing of significance in our regard. Subsequently, I was rehired twice and phased out twice, as the state and college's fiscal status determined my own fate. In September 1999, I was rehired in an adjunct capacity.

Let me make clear that the tenure track faculty and departmental support staff I worked with were, in nearly every instance, fine and congenial colleagues, thoroughly professional in every respect, making my job as enjoyable as possible. And the students, especially in my last position, were, if not always initially eager and willing to learn, certainly largely receptive to my efforts to engage them and spur their interest in the subject matter.

When I originally submitted this piece, I honestly believed I would never return to academia. Then, unexpectedly, I received two teaching job offers within a month. I chose to return to a situation and environment I knew well, and despite considerable administrative turmoil, I have no regrets.

Looking back, I'm not sure what I would have done differently. It does not take much to see your chances for any position in academia derailed due to a less than laudatory letter of recommendation or personal evaluation, or some real or perceived slight directed at a key decision-maker. Maybe the best option involves cultivating the proper mentor so that your career will be shepherded on a magic carpet ride, ascending effortlessly to a position atop the greasy pole.

I love to use an athletic analogy when thinking of my career in academia, likening it to the record of a veteran minor league baseball player who did a solid, workmanlike job when he got the chance to play in "The Show," but somehow got caught in a numbers or dollars game and never could stay there long enough or play regularly to win a regular paying job. Until now.

Will I Pass the Test?

by Erica Werner

A few weeks ago, I asked my college composition students to help me make a list of words or phrases they like to use, ones that upon reaching the eyes or ears, make them feel good. We were working on the importance of recognizing the connotations of words, along with the effective use of specifics in descriptions.

A pleasant sounding collection quickly accumulated: they gave me words such as "charisma," "erotica," "superfluous," "gecko pimento," whatever that means, "onomatopoeia" and others. Next, the ugly words. I had to get them started on this one. As freshmen, they weren't too secure about uttering derogatory terms or gross body functions to the person responsible for their grades. "You know, like 'pus,'" I said.

They groaned.

Their reaction spurred me on. "'Sardine'…'Diarrhea,' " I explained.

They moaned again, even louder.

Inspired, I continued. "Like 'Adjunct'"

Their lack of response this time confused me. I turned from the chalkboard with what must have been a puzzled look on my face. "But what's wrong with THAT one?" a young woman finally asked.

At that moment, it struck me that my own adverse reaction to that word is not universal. It is especially not duplicated in naive young college students who think that degrees are their tickets to independence and success, who also believe that all of their professors are comfortable and satisfied, able to devote endless amounts of energy to helping them achieve the same. "Never mind," I said. "I'll tell you some other time."

That word, for the most part, does trouble me. Adjunct means a secondary or nonessential addition. As my job position is classified as an adjunct instructor, that definition alone is most certainly an insult. I teach at two respected colleges, and at neither am I a secondary or non-essential addition. I cover the same material as full-time professors, and without the presence of adjuncts at both institutions, classes would have to be cancelled. But there's much more to this word than is revealed by examining the standard definition. There's nothing in it about the anger, the disappointment, the frustration and the depression that for me and many others go hand-in-hand with its collegiate usage. Nor does it mention the amount of growth that has occurred in me as a direct result of becoming an "adjunct" instructor.

Teaching is a career I fell into. I use that cliché—fell into—with purpose. For me, it's been similar to falling in love, gaining mutual respect and compatibility at breakneck speed. Also, just like falling in love, the longer one is with her partner, the more apparent flaws and irritants become. Some disenchantment is bound to occur. At some point, one must make conscious decisions: is the relationship worth the work involved? Is compromise worthwhile? Does the love outweigh the pain, or vice versa?

After four years of being an adjunct, I have much for which to be thankful. I have gained valuable experience teaching numerous courses for several different sizes and types of colleges and universities. I'm proud of the progress made by both my students and myself.

Four years ago, Master's Degree in Creative Writing fresh in the cardboard roll in which it had been sent, I worked full-time as a technical assistant in the library of the university from which I had graduated. I earned more at that job than I do now, teaching college English. I needed the money, so I applied for a part-time teaching job listed in the newspaper. Three days before the fall semester was to begin, I was called for an interview. My visit to the gas station bathroom a block from the college to freshen up after the 50-mile drive was longer than my time spent in the dean's office. Though I had no teaching experience, had not yet seen the textbooks, was shy to the point of obvious discomfort, and had mediocre college transcripts, I was hired on the spot.

Though it was terrifying at the time, I'm now grateful for that opportunity. Thank goodness that first class contained the perfect chemistry: a great bunch of kind, conscientious adult students who were all older than me, and who seemed to look upon me as the non-threatening, enthusiastic "expert"/kid that I was. I quickly decided that I needed to do this job full-time and was forced to lose my fear of speaking to people; to become an advocate, counselor, mentor and educator all wrapped up into one; to teach MYSELF how to teach. I did, and am still doing all of that. But what if I hadn't? What if I had been terrible at it, unwilling or unable to figure out what to do? No assistance was given to me. The freedom was nice, but I could have also used some help and support. If I had been an inadequate teacher, the students would have wasted their time and money and might not have been equipped as writers for the rest of their college careers.

The salary has been heart-breaking, a source of many stressful periods in my life. Last year, I taught six three-hour classes in the spring, four in the summer and seven in the fall—six different courses on four campuses. I felt like I was running a one-woman school for beginning writers. In addition to hours spent in the classroom, this required tremendous amounts of planning, grading, conferencing and driving time (with no travel allowance). Before taxes, I made $15,000. I figured out that I made $2.12 an hour. Though I've changed colleges, the rate of pay is still about the same. The secretaries in the English departments make more than I do. At least graduate students who are teaching assistants get free tuition in addition to their meager salaries. I can't pay my more than $300 per month in student loans. It's sad and ironic that I teach, at the minimum, a full-time load of college courses, and I am unable to repay the loans that got me here. Traveling, movies, magazines, new clothes, having a telephone in my house and going to the doctor are all infrequent luxuries. At the schools I'm at now, my students eat better, dress better, and drive better cars than I do. And most of them do not work at a job.

There are other difficult aspects of an adjunct's life. We receive no health insurance, sick or vacation time, or benefits of any kind. We usually are assigned the classes that the full-timers don't want—early in the morning or late at night (and boy, are we lucky to get them). I have no job security. Two of my six classes were cancelled at the last minute this past summer; hence my anticipated salary for the three-month period was instantly reduced by $1,800. Never have I known such fear or panic.

Attitudes toward adjuncts are not often pleasant, either. Though the same quality of work, amount of education and devotion are expected from me as from the full-time teachers, I do not always receive the amount of respect from them that I feel I deserve. Once, in a heated personal discussion with a full-time colleague, she blurted out, "Who the hell do you think you are? You're only an adjunct here!" Initially, this comment stunned and hurt me. But soon, anger and indignation took over. During the semester this was said to me, I was teaching nearly twice the load that this person was for half the salary. It's not right for me to be judged upon what I receive for the job instead of on what I have to give to it.

Again, this is not always true. Some full-time colleagues have expressed sympathy and understanding, as they too were once in my position. This I do appreciate, but their kind words and encouragement alone do not help me or the many others like me. I can't count the number of times I have accidentally walked in on a party or meeting to which I was not invited when I've gone to check my mailbox in the teachers' lounge. My presence is simply ignored. I myself am powerless. If I express dissatisfaction, I'm afraid of being dismissed or simply dropped from the teaching roster for the next semester. There are hordes of other educated people who are qualified for and willing to do my job.

So what do I say to students who ask my advice on whether or not to go into the teaching profession? I tell them that it's the most rewarding job I've ever had or ever will have. It's also been the most difficult. I tell them to either become qualified to teach in the public schools, or to continue straight through to earn Ph.D.s. I tell them that they had better be completely dedicated to serving, that they'll have to be able to ignore all the hardships and focus on the job itself. Then, if that doesn't deter them, I tell them my salary. If they're thinking about this profession, that's something they need to know.

Because of all of these factors, I feel like I'm always trying to catch up on the things that are most important to me. Catch up on bills and money owed that I have borrowed to survive. Catch up on sleep. Catch up on my own writing. Catch up on precious time spent with my partner. Catch up on the never-ending supply of student papers. Unfortunately, the only one of these that I'm ever successful at accomplishing is my schoolwork.

In spite of my many complaints, I view this experience primarily as a positive one. Because of my own lonely time spent as a student, I strive to be the teacher I didn't have, and I get to see the rewards of that every day. The more pressure I'm under, the more inspired I become, both as a teacher and as a writer. When I'm burdened with responsibilities, particularly at the end of the semester, so many new ideas come to me. Working intensely with young writers during the day, and then being up at two in the morning with purple grading pen in hand, good music on the stereo, cigarette smoke a haze in the lonely room surrounded by black outside, is conducive to that. Under these circumstances, ideas are rich and plentiful; time to develop them is a rare, valuable commodity.

My definition of work-related success is forever altered. To me now, success at work will be being able to do this for the rest of my life while getting paid a decent wage. I have learned what my true passions are. For this, I consider myself immeasurably fortunate. I have learned how to block out the negative when I need to and concentrate on what I love—the job itself. I have learned that I strongly have it in me to be devoted, committed, to endure. In a continual cycle of shared growth and learning, I help students, and they in turn help me. And it's not just about grammar and about proper writing technique: those things are catalysts towards powerful expression, openness, acceptance and internal growth for all of us.

I see this difficult time as an internship. But how long will this interim period last? I have no way of knowing. I only hope that someday soon, somebody with clout in an English department will smile and say to me, "Enter. You have passed the test."

I wrote the previous pages of this essay three years ago. Now I have a phone and health benefits. I also have another more-than-full-time job with the US Postal Service, in addition to remaining an adjunct instructor. I type addresses into a computer all day in a job that requires fast, accurate fingers and a high school diploma. My salary has doubled while my belief in the value of a liberal arts education has, at times, dwindled. Everything else remains the same.

I haven't been an activist. I haven't joined a union. I've always had the hope that once somebody saw what a good teacher I am, noticed how devoted I am to this profession, that good things would follow. That faith has also wavered. What HAS kept me here, doing this job when I am no longer financially dependent upon it, are my experiences with students.

This semester is almost finished: one class left. In three hectic hours on my day off from the post office, I met with fifteen students to talk about their research papers. Jeff, a junior accounting major who had postponed taking freshman English until he absolutely had to, asked me whom I would recommend that he take for Intro to Lit next fall. "I learned so much this semester. I never thought that I'd like English, but I love it now. I want to take somebody next term who teaches like you do," he said.

The intensity in his sincere eyes, and the feeling that only I could have done that for him, and damn, did I do it well--that's why I'm still here.

Though I'm not sure how long I can keep it up.

We Only Come out at Night

by Will MacKenzie

There is much agonizing and hand wringing over the plight of adjunct faculty. There is no doubt that they are treated poorly, as are all at the lower tiers of an economy where benefits are tied to full employment, and the drudgery of dealing daily most directly with most people is left to the least well compensated. But there are also great rewards from the role.

I need to state that I have not had to make my living, support my family, or build a future upon my role as an adjunct, so for me it has been an occasional role, something which allowed me to pursue something I enjoyed, something I do better than the average, and which gives me an arena where I can test ideas without risk. I am not bucking for promotion, aiming to build a CV, or worm my way to the center of the academic nest. From this perspective, working as an adjunct has provided an interesting view into academia, allowed me to implement my own vision of teaching, and clarified much of what is important and what is dross in education, especially at the entry level where adjuncts labor and their students greet them. This personal essay will lay out the dark side of the adjunct life to exorcise those demons, then look at the brighter aspects, not to justify the practices, but more to demonstrate that there is something larger to teaching than the academic drudges and pettifogging, well paid, smug administrators that makes being an adjunct fun. For without us, higher education would shut down. (To be fair to other academic laborers, I should include TAs, the grad student kind, in the mix of those exploited. However, grad students make a Faustian bargain and gain something in their servitude.)

My first adjunct experience came on the heels of an unexpected death of a chairman. Often adjuncts are brought into the breech. The shuffling of courses by the chair or course coordinator to cover the sudden absence always involves just one too many rearrangements, temptations to break earlier promises to permanent faculty, or the dreaded setting of precedent, which in the collegial academic atmosphere has as much, or more, power than law. I had never applied for the position I was being offered. I think my name must have come from the chair's Rolodex or stack of business cards he had collected when we had met at a conference. In sales lingo, my recruitment was a "cold call." As common, I was given the only courses unfilled, two night sessions. I was glad for the work as I was making the transition from active duty military service to civilian life. My contract was renewed for the spring. This time only one course, which suited me well, as I had just taken a new full time position in academic administration—well paid, full benefits, and smug.

The stint as an adjunct, however, had teased me. The administrative position I had taken was less rewarding than I had expected, with the hierarchies between faculty and staff as sharp as any between the officer's mess and enlisted chow hall. I had lived both sides of that divide, where rank was worn on a sleeve, but I struggled with the treachery and invisible rank that fueled small academic intrigue.

In mid-spring at the college where I was teaching, I sat with the chair, a woman of great earnestness, to glean advice about a possible permanent position, or the route to take for such a position. As an adjunct, I had learned new pleasures in running my own class.

Now, some fifteen years later, I realize my naiveté in asking for a meeting as a position had been advertised. I had been given no word of it. My asking for advice put the chair, for whom I was just a temporary plug, in an uncomfortable position. It had already been decided that my time of service was done.

From this first experience, I learned that adjuncts do not get the mentoring that is so critical to building an academic career. The very simple "where tos" and "how tos" of publishing, the rules as to what is really a publication and what is not, a review of an academic record, a way to build on strengths or any form of career advice are all missing. Even the simple offer of a permanent position is often not made. This lack of a larger identity with future prospects makes moving out of the labors in the lower rungs difficult, made more difficult by an absence of written guidelines and powered by personal networks. Is it better to not be told of a permanent job opening than to be told and passed over for it? You fill the temp slot, then vanish.

My next adjunct position was quite different. Again it was on short-term notice; this time, at the institution I was working for as an administrator. The position was as one half of a team-taught course. Again, it was at night. I was mercy companion to a mercy position for a faculty member, fallen from the pinnacle of a deanship, on his way out, and one step from his next failed academic job to a teetering career as a consultant. No colleague would teach with him. He couldn't, likely wouldn't, teach alone—not in the contract.

For our team, I alone had to prepare the biweekly quizzes, both questions and answers; vett them with my partner; duplicate, collate, administer, grade and record them. After the second lecture as we walked back to our offices, my partner asked soto-voce, if I were terminally qualified. At that time, the answer was, "No". He suggested that it would be proper for me to call him "Dr. Weston," and he would call me "Professor MacKenzie", if we were to address each other in the classroom. (Neither the name nor the gender should be taken as representative of this particular individual. The use of "he" is in its neutral singular reference; "it" would not be polite.)

Besides my clerical labors with the quizzes and other course paraphernalia, there was a unique concept to team teaching. I could be interrupted. He could not. I could deliver my hour's lecture, to be followed by his presentation with its opening statement that contradicted the entire argument I had labored for the prior hour to build. Ignoring discussions that we'd had before class, this came as much more a surprise to me than to our students. They had not had the benefit of a prior meeting where we reviewed the day's topic and our respective approaches. The students quickly grew used to our different styles. Some had even taken to arriving only for the second half if they knew Dr. Weston was the lead act, pleading a work or family conflict for their tardiness.

The *coup de grace* came at term's end with the course evaluations. My partner blithely said, as a tenured professor, he would not be evaluated. It was not required by contract. Only I, unappointed let alone untenured, would have to have the students evaluate me. The students, who had anticipated this moment and hoped to comment on our respective merits as instructors, were stunned. They had no recourse except by public complaint to express their satisfaction or dissatisfaction with the teaching. It was a curious way for the students to learn that the capricious rules of academia do not start and stop with distribution requirements which can no longer be met, or obscure courses taught by only one professor one semester, whose sabbatical is not made public until he is gone.

At Dr. Weston's request, I joined him to teach the second semester of the year long course. With fifteen weeks companionship to our credit, we dropped the pretense of being a team, and taught what we chose, how we chose, often not bothering to attend the other's presentation. Our mutual absences began first with the excuses of a board meeting, or children's events, but gradually just petered out. I still prepared, administered, and graded the quizzes. I alone was again evaluated, but this time students wrote notes expressing their frustration over this. At year's end, with school loans repaid by the adjunct gig, I retired from adjunct teaching. Not that I wasn't asked. Again, the chair of another department at the same school asked if I would teach.

Again it was short notice, this time, only less than 48 hours before the start of the term. I said no, arguing that if a professional job was to be done, then more consideration needed to be given. I did offer, in exchange, to teach a more senior course, where the enrollment was smaller, in a subject area I had taught before so it would be modifying a course, not creating one from whole cloth. This would free a permanent faculty, who had taught the proffered course before, to switch and take up the open position. The "emergency," however, was not sufficient to overcome the status differential between the entry level and vaunted arena of upper division courses. Adjuncts could labor at the base of the pyramid, but the Coptic eye, with its vision, wisdom and knowledge, was only a privilege of the ranked staff.

After a two or three year hiatus, I again was approached for teaching. The academic program in which I'd had so many interesting team-teaching adventures was being phased out. Only those students who had enrolled under a set of rules from the late eighties were still required to take the course. These students, like the adjuncts, were the part-timers, those with families and day jobs, who would spend six, eight, or sometimes ten years in completing a bachelor's degree. My partner, a former administrator who retired from administrative duties, and I were to assume the professorship, which went with this posting. We were the ones who would fold the tent. A dying program, taught by the invisible, with no expectation of success or failure, represented academic freedom like none seen before or since.

I have never had a more ideal teaching experience. It seemed that so long as there wasn't a complaint from students, the course could be structured as we wanted, use whatever texts we wanted, and be conducted as we best saw fit. My partner this time 'round wasn't about to do any heavy lifting. His position, while permanent, was worse than any adjunct's. He got the left over courses of left over courses in a department seemingly shamed that he had dropped in among their midst, without their choice, and taken up a tenured spot. He was demeaned by the senior department faculty and despised by the junior, but he was a fixture. He, however, was a great partner, and we split the bar bill evenly. This was a true partnership where our teaching began to take a mutually supportive role, where we taught from our strengths, dividing the topics in uniquely personal ways, learning from each other as the students learned from us.

Hiring outsiders as a result of "national searches" seems to be code words for safe out-placements, judging by their competencies in practice rather than on paper. Since my primary employment was as an academic administrator--lower tier, frozen in position--I wandered from a college to a university. Status differences at the university between staff and faculty were much more clear. There didn't seem to be the competition or the struggles between the two groups as at the earlier, smaller institution. Perhaps it was the presence of graduate students who played whipping boy as the lowest tier. Competition within the administrative ranks was vicious and more than compensated for faculty charity.

The university used no adjuncts in the day-laborer sense of the colleges. They had internal mechanisms of a librarian or semi-employed scholarly editor, whose jobs were fleshed out with a course here or there. The few undisguised professional courses (mostly of a business ilk, such as Introduction to Finance) were taught off schedule, usually in the evening, and were led by downtown practitioners from the Big Eight or nationally ranked law firms. Nosing around, one could find appointments as "lecturer" who had academic or research jobs elsewhere or an internal academic administrative position who taught a course or two. But the adjunct contract was not part of the university scene.

This environment there did not seem to offer the opportunities for adjuncts that there had been at earlier institutions. But the casual labor train knows no restraint. Here the institutionally accepted and promoted arena was the non-credit adult ed or enrichment program. The university advertised this as a community service, when it was as much a matter of efficient use of otherwise empty space. This was a purely commercial arena, without pretensions to a higher purpose. The compensation for classroom time was better than the adjunct life because there was no homework, no assignments to prepare, grade and record. The students either "got it" during the classroom hours or not. There were no degrees, credits, grades.

There was no pretension to offices, academic support, or career development. It was "market place" teaching as pure and platonic as Socrates. These positions were dangled to department employees as a perk, to make up for naturally depressed, or uncompetitive, academic salaries. They were traded among employees. If favored in the department, taking on these courses reflected well on your performance evaluation, and a blind eye was turned to work time you might use to meet the course obligations. If unfavored in the administrative department and by some fluke a course came your way, all effort was made to have you pass the opportunity to someone more deserving. The pettiness of the administrative ranks was a learned skill, from those more valued in the faculty ranks. This group had taken only what they could apply in the hopes of giving themselves "academic value."

Again I have changed my permanent position, now moving closer to working with teachers in secondary schools and high schools. There is, however, little change throughout the educational system. If adjuncts find themselves lacking rewards and poorly compensated, try substitute teaching, which will send anyone to the poorhouse if not the asylum. The giddyingly amusing circumstances, such as being called upon to teach indoor archery to special education students, and the struggles against the enmity of teenagers who, if aggressive see you as merely something to be broken, like a horse, or if sullen, see you as something to be endured, are hardly roles where you can make a difference.

Teaching, direct contact with students, is not valued. It is something people do for pleasure. Rewards remove teachers from teaching and draw teachers from the classroom to administration or research. In the world we have built, we do not value direct contact. The lower tiers of all professions, waiters in the restaurant, nurses in the hospital, tellers at the bank, and house keeping staff at the hotel, are all your human contact in institutions. For all of these people, there are rewards that transcend the compensation, the abuse, and the exploitation built into the systems and structures that govern the institutions. To truly celebrate humanity, to revel in its variety, to puzzle over differences in understanding, to suddenly see the world through a different set of eyes, to have your preconceptions challenged, takes a calling. It is listening to that other voice that makes the great teachers. It is that other voice that gives you strength to schlep the bags from the parking lot to the classroom in a miserable New

England winter. It is that other voice that you learn to rely on for counsel and support, not the chair's, not the academic peer, not the academic administrator. It is your voice against all sense and rational choice that moves you to accept, again, a position at night.

The Lonely Run of the Adjunct Instructor

by Paul Yovino

This story is true. The facts presented are true, but the name of the institution has been omitted--to protect the guilty. These are the reflections of an adjunct instructor who no longer has any connection with this south of Boston suburban college, but who wished for that college to remain viable. However, if this recent experience with this institution is any indication, its viability is in serious question.

I had been teaching Speech and Mass Communication for several years as an adjunct at this college. Each semester, I am proud to note, my classes were at or beyond capacity enrollment. I took it as a high honor that students who had taken my course recommended it to their fellow students because they gained so much from it.

In particular, I found it rewarding that so many international students, a large part of the student body, encouraged other international students to enroll because the course helped them to more easily adjust to English as their second language and to succeed in their other courses at the college. It was equally gratifying to watch the progress of one or two local students each semester who overcame what they at first believe to be an insurmountable fear of public speaking.

With this success in mind, I found it incomprehensible to understand why after all these years, I was replaced by a more politically connected person who had never taught those courses. The administration, an oxymoron in and of itself, attempted to address this situation with the legalism that as an adjunct, one teaches at the college from one semester contract to another; that is a given. To use that as an explanation works about as well as Al Gore's explanation earlier regarding his fund raising activities that no controlling legal authority applied. That is a legalism, not an explanation.

Let me review what I believe to be some very odd occurrences that transpired during my last semester at the school. I had taught two summer school sessions at the college through the early part of August. My second summer class was held in a room that should never have been used as a classroom since it did not have a chalkboard, a white board or even an overhead projector for class lectures. Several weeks into the term, I asked the Vice President of Educational Services (this person was well connected to the community political structure to whom she owed her job) if I could have a portable chalkboard until a more permanent arrangement could be made.

Frankly, I was not prepared for this person's angry and inappropriate response. This woman, who bore a striking resemblance to Rosie ODonnell, yelled at me, in front of a group of students, that I would just have to put up with it. Beyond her angry outburst, I was more concerned that this college vice president would allow such an inadequate room to be used as a classroom and would ever question an instructor's effort to rectify the college's mistake and embarrass an instructor in front of students. It demonstrates a clear lack of respect for both the instructor and for the students who paid full tuition for 100% of the instructor's effort and full tuition for 100% of the college's effort. If I did not speak out, I would hope that one of my students would demand another classroom or a tuition refund. Still, it is this vice president's response that I should dare to ask for the basics in my classroom that remains with me as some Dickensian image of

Oliver Twist asking for more gruel in the orphanage! Nonetheless, this summer class was one of my most productive--because I made it so.

As the summer class was coming to an end, I met with the chair of my department, and she thanked me for my efforts and proceeded to present me with my fall semester schedule. In addition, she asked me if I might be available to teach any other courses if the need arose. There was absolutely no indication from her that I would not be rehired for the fall, and she again thanked me for the help and encouragement I had given her in her new position. What a difference a few days made when I called the chair to ask her when I would receive my contract for the fall semester. She paused, and then told me, "We are not going to use you this semester." Of course, she immediately recited the legalism that I was just an adjunct, which as I mentioned before is not an explanation. I asked her if there had been some problem with my teaching, but she went on praise it. Suspecting that the vice president's combative attitude over the board may have precipitated this action, I pressed my department chair for a greater explanation. She resorted to the easy out of legalisms again.

More disconcerting, however, was the fact that she did not know who was replacing me. When I reminded her that as chair of the department knowing her instructors was basic information, she told me that I was harassing her and hung up on me. Subsequently, I placed a call to the Vice President of Educational Services who also spouted the same legalism without further explanation. Odd, isn't it? I am praised one minute; given a fall schedule the next and the very day before fall classes are to start, I am told sorry, someone else is teaching that class; you are just an adjunct.

As this college has come to rely more and more on just adjuncts, one would think that the college would attempt to maintain some degree of stability and continuity in a subject matter by retaining as many qualified adjuncts as possible. Evidently, this college cares less about those factors and is content to have any warm body that just might look like an instructor in the classroom. Students pay too much at this institution to have expensive baby sitters.

Perhaps, the college's inability to communicate is symptomatic of its greater problems, and an experience I'd had at the college long before my final summer there verifies that. Although I was only an adjunct at this college, I previously had been asked by the president to prepare a program proposal for the expansion of the college's communication curriculum because so many students wished to pursue careers in communication. After his invitation, I wrote to the president of the college to congratulate him on the announced partnership between the college and a large supermarket chain, which would use the college as an employee training facility, and I said that I would be pleased to meet with him to develop a Speech Communications in The Workplace curriculum for this new partnership if this would not duplicate any other efforts.

In support of that proposal, I noted to the president that the Massachusetts College of Communication, MCC, in Boston had nearly tripled its enrollment in two years because of the demand from a wide array of students for communication courses. It was at that time that I prepared a detailed proposal to establish the program I called the MIC--The Massachusetts Institute of Communications Program. It outlined objectives, staff, cost and curriculum. I even met with the owner of a local radio station who was more than willing to work with the college to defray costs and to help establish a college radio station on a vacant FM frequency.

All the extra work I did was done without any monetary compensation whatsoever, but college personnel continued to drop hints that I would be the one chosen to manage the college radio station.

How was this proposal met? I never received any acknowledgment of my efforts, and my calls and visits to the presidents were ignored--even though he had initially asked me to do this work. Then, after more than a year of work and after having made great progress in establishing a college radio station, the president of the college eliminated the Communications Major from the curriculum without warning or consultation. Students who now sought a communications curriculum at this college were turned away, and those students went elsewhere. The fact that *The Boston Sunday Globe* reported that a student of this college withdrew and went on to Massachusetts College of Communication to pursue a now successful communications career had no effect on the president. As the reporter for the *Globe* stated, it is to MCC that [this woman] gives credit for her professional success. And I add, not to this college.

The question that must be asked is why did she have to go to MCC, and why was she not able to give credit for her professional success to this college. I cannot give a rational answer to the president's irrational action.

There are--or perhaps were--people willing and able to help this college succeed. Just like me they have been pushed aside, dismissed, ignored and generally been made to feel unwelcome. They are looked upon with suspicion and distrust if not total resentment by those who believe they and they alone are the college, and anyone who attempts to help the college must be out for their jobs and must be disqualified. As enrollment at this college continues to drop and drop precipitously, will these same individuals take the responsibility for the demise of the college. I do not think so. Even now I am sure they are looking for new scapegoats, but unlike Casablanca, there are no more usual suspects; they are all gone.

The old adage warns to be kind to the people you meet on your way up because you will need them on your way down. It applies here, and it applies to the now former college president who chose to find a position out of state because of some irregularities in the college finances. Still, the cronies and hacks remain in control, and the hand picked successor to the former president jumps at their commands.

It appears that this college will, within a matter of time, fall under the weight of gross mismanagement and political patronage at its worst. I hope the original founders of this institution are no longer among the living, for to watch the demise of their college would surely kill them.

In a final defense of adjunct instructors, I will note that some of the brightest and finest individuals I have met were adjuncts. They are usually experts in their field of endeavor, and because of that, they bring a wealth of experience to the classroom that a tenured instructor cannot. Nonetheless, or perhaps because of this, they are seen as threats to teacher unions and administrations alike. Neither can control them, and in an institution as fraught with political hacks as this college, that was anathema.

On a less humorous note, this past winter I received a call from the college asking me to alter the grade of a student. She had dropped out of my class after the first day, but now she needed the grade to graduate. I will let your imagination wander on what I told them they could do.

And so, my stay at this place of higher learning came to an abrupt end. I was replaced by a crony who I later found out hardly appeared to teach her class. Perhaps she was afraid to speak in public...

Rock the Boat

by Ed Meek

According to recent figures, male college graduates in the United States will earn an average of $61,000 per year over the course of their career. That figure is a few thousand less than what full-time college faculty earn. Last year, teaching five courses per semester and two intensive courses in the summer (a full time load at the two colleges where I teach consists of three to four classes per semester), serving on two committees, serving as faculty advisor on two undergraduate publications, coordinating a Freshman Seminar Program and advising a handful of students, I made $30,000. Of course, I don't just have one college degree. I have a B.A. in English, a Master's of Fine Arts in Creative Writing, and I am currently enrolled in an English M.A. program in Composition Studies. My students say in evaluations I am an excellent teacher. My bosses would love to hire me, but their hands are tied. They have money in their budget for computers and computer staff, for new buildings and for financial personnel, but they claim it's a matter of tight budgets and an excessive supply of well-trained people who are willing to do what I do. "You are a dime a dozen" one of my bosses once said.

Charles Dickens could not have envisioned this situation—a professional class of part-time and adjunct college faculty who teach approximately half of the courses offered in the colleges and universities in America, who are paid less than half what their full-time counterparts earn, who often have no retirement benefits, no health insurance and no job security. At one of the schools at which I teach, a small Catholic liberal arts college, we are, in fact, called "part-time temporary employees" on the contracts they send us in the mail every January and August. We are not included in faculty raises or in discussions of benefits. We are, in short, ignored by both the full-time faculty and the administration.

I've been teaching part-time now for twelve years. I've been assured, promised and told by a number of deans and English Department heads that I would be hired full-time. At one of the schools at which I teach, I have been interviewed for five different openings. I was, in fact, voted on and recommended to the dean by the search committee and the Division of Humanities for a tenure track slot, but in a Byzantine series of events stemming from another part-timer (a woman) threatening to sue the college for sexual discrimination were they to hire me, the dean was advised by the college lawyer to give the position to a woman from outside the college in order to avoid the suit. I was hired by this same college full-time on a one-year contract for another position; a year later, budget cuts included the cutting of this position. I was promised I would be re-hired the following year, but when the time came, I was told, "Perhaps next year."

Deans make over $100,000 a year; department heads over $60,000. The only way to enable them to be paid the way they are paid is to have part-timers and adjuncts who make $10,000-$20,000 per year teaching classes. After all, administrators have their priorities. Parents and students expect and demand gyms and weight rooms and decent food in the cafeteria. They expect and get an entire staff of student service personnel with counselors and medical staff and student activities people and residence advisors. In addition, we need more and more computers, personnel to teach us and our students how to use them, and technicians to fix them and help us when we get stuck. We need more deans to run the growing Evening Division, to coordinate the student services people, to develop and run new graduate programs, to handle our burgeoning technology needs.

Although administrators and faculty regularly give lip service to the importance of teaching at the college level, ultimately, teaching matters little to them. They are in the business of selling seats to students and to the parents of students. They need all of the above to sell those seats, and they need faculty with terminal degrees who do research and publish in arcane journals so that Admissions can use them as marketing tools.

Full-time faculty are unwitting co-conspirators in the exploitation of part-timers. They are paid what they are paid, and they receive the benefits they receive, in large part because we are paid less than half of what they are paid, and because we receive few, if any benefits. One of the Orwellian aspects of this situation is the way in which full-time faculty resent part-timers. They see us as transients who are not as qualified, who are never around, who do not help out with the committee work or with the advising. They may, in a vague sense, feel pity for us, but we have not worked as hard as they have, and we are not as deserving or as privileged. Although they would like to see us paid a little more, given more benefits, they are not willing to risk what they have fought and worked so hard to attain. That is, they are not willing to stand in solidarity with us because they do not see us as one of them.

There are other places to levy blame of course: graduate schools which turn out students when there are few positions to be filled; government for not supporting state schools, causing endless rounds of cutbacks in faculty and staff, the results of laissez faire capitalism which allows supply and demand to exploit people and weaken our educational system.

So what do we do about it? First, we must let people know what the situation is. Parents should know that they are not getting what they are paying for. They are not getting the kind of support and commitment from part-time temporary personnel that they would be getting from full-time faculty. We have to remind full-time faculty that it is in their interests to support our cause since, if we were full-time, we could help share in the responsibilities of running the college. We have to let deans know that although they may be responsible for selling students the seats in our classroom, we are the ones responsible for keeping the students in those seats until they graduate. We are the ones preparing our students to succeed in the world. After all, it is only if we do our job well that those students will contribute to the college endowment. We have to let students know that they are not getting what they, and their parents, are paying for. Finally, at some point, we have to engage in praxis by taking a stand, individually and collectively. We must refuse to teach classes for $1,000 or $2,000 per semester, no benefits included. We have to stop deluding ourselves into thinking that eventually administrators and other faculty will recognize the good work we do and will reward us for it.

There are many directions higher education can take in the coming years. The Division of Continuing Education may take over. We will have much more distance learning, flex-time, off-site classes. As education changes, there will be opportunities for changing the way we think of part-time and full-time faculty. Many of those who teach part-time who have become integral faculty members at colleges must be hired full-time. Those who have become permanent part-time faculty should be hired half-time. All faculty, part-time or full-time, should have access to benefits. At the very least, part-time faculty ought to be able to buy into benefit plans. Pay per course ought to be pro-rated. That means part-time faculty ought to be paid between $3,500 and $5,000 (today's dollars) per class. Finally, part-time faculty should have the right to be promoted and rewarded if they do good work. As one union official once said to me, "My experience is when you step on someone's toes, they back off."

We have to begin stepping on other people's toes.

The Censorship of Part-Timers

by Martin Naparsteck

A part-time faculty member is paid typically one-fourth to one-third of what a full-timer gets for teaching a course, usually receives few or no fringe benefits, and has virtually no chance of ever getting a sabbatical, tenure or promotion. Everyone knows part-timers are the most openly exploited class on America's college campuses. The only trouble is, if you're a part-timer and you say what everyone knows, you're likely to lose your job. That's what happened to me at one of the colleges I worked at in New York.

I taught part-time at a total of nine colleges for eighteen years. For eleven years, I taught part-time in a college in upstate New York.

After I had been there eight years, I became active within the union that represents faculty in this system. I wrote articles in my chapter's newsletter and for the daily newspapers in the city where I taught, letters to the editor of *The Chronicle of Higher Education* and elsewhere criticizing the college and the university for its treatment of part-timers with the same message.

I was becoming effective in getting the union to reform itself so it would better represent the interests of part-timers. For example, I got the union to adopt a resolution that, for the first time in its then two-decade old history, committed it to fighting as hard to protect the jobs of part timers as it does those of full-timers. I wrote a position paper that became part of union policy—the union, with 22,000 members, is the largest higher education unit in the nation—that called on the state to give part-timers tenure, sabbaticals and real opportunities for promotion.

I wrote an op-ed article that appeared in both dailies in the city where I worked—they had a combined circulation of nearly a quarter of a million—that criticized the system and particularly my college for their treatment of part-timers.

It was no secret in the college that the president was enraged with me. At a faculty meeting, he berated me in front of two dozen colleagues; another time, he openly ridiculed a letter I had published in *The Chronicle of HigherEducation* about part-timers.

When the school system ordered that cuts be made for budgetary reasons, I was axed, even though I had been with the college longer than more than half of its full-timers, had better student evaluations than almost all of them and taught in areas of high student demand, creative writing and journalism.

When I filed a grievance through the union, the college officially said the reason I was let go was because it no longer needed anyone to teach a creative writing course where I taught; the college said that even though it hired someone else to teach creative writing there even before my dismissal took effect.

After the president fired me, I continued to write my articles, including those for the chapter newsletter. The president's reaction was to suggest to the president of the chapter that it not print all of the articles it receives, a view the chapter president did not accept.

While my grievance proceeded slowly through the university bureaucracy, I had to teach elsewhere. Among the places I taught since being censored by firing at my college was a community college in the same city. Several part-timers there, familiar with my articles in the local press, talked to me about upcoming contract negotiations. They noted that the faculty union had a negotiations team that consisted entirely of full-timers, even though about half the faculty was made up of part-timers. They wanted to know if I would do something to help. I agreed. I wrote letters and articles and spoke to union officials, and the union agreed to allow an advisory part-timer to sit in some negotiations meetings. But what struck me was this: to bolster my arguments, I circulated a petition in which part-timers demanded the union and college treat them better. Dozens and dozens of part-timers signed it; dozens of full-timers signed a related support petition. But many part-timers told me that while they agreed with the petition called for, they didn't want to sign it. Some noted that they could damage their families by not being rehired the next semester. Some used clichés like not wanting to make waves. Some said they had heard what had happened to me. Later, the community college fired me because of my outspokenness on behalf of part-timers.

The message is as clear in New York as it is around the nation. If you're a part-timer, you don't speak up about the way colleges exploit you. If you do, you get axed.

Adjunct Apartheid

by Barbara Wilson Hahn

S pring is a lovely time of year in the Southwest. Days are warm enough for short sleeves and picnics. Five years ago, coming down the path from the library on one such fine spring day, I noticed several of the tenured faculty milling around the entrance to the snack bar at the small community college where I'd been hired as an adjunct instructor in the English Department. Tables covered with white linen cloths had been set up outside under the ramada between the snack bar and the administrative offices. I was headed for the office of the Activities Director, which was housed in a room just west of the eating area and snack bar. Closing the AD's door behind me, I asked, "What's up?"

"The faculty picnic," she answered. "Would you look at that table of goodies?"

A long table against the east wall of the snack bar was loaded with chips and dips; deli trays of meats and cheeses; crackers; rolls; brown and white breads; vegetable trays; several pitchers containing iced tea, lemonade, and coffee; and some scrumptious cookies and cakes. Underneath the table, a tub of ice housed soft drinks of many varieties.

"Yum!" I said. "I'm really hungry. C'mon, let's get us a plate before it all disappears."

"You aren't invited," the AD said, "and neither am I."

"Why not?" I asked over the sudden growling of my stomach.

"It's only for full-time faculty," she said with a tinge of bitterness I found unusual for her. She was generally fun loving, upbeat and positive.

"That's rotten. Did you try to go through the line?" I asked, still holding onto the hope that she was mistaken, and that she wasn't invited, not because she was part-time but because she was the Activities Director, and not technically "faculty."

"Jim, the adjunct from the art department, is in the administrative office setting up the art show. He came in on his own time to set it up, and he came over a little bit ago and wanted a cola from the tub because he was hot. They told him the drinks were for full-time faculty only, and he'd have to buy his from the snack bar."

Turning Jim away made it clear that adjunct faculty members were unwelcome at the luncheon. The tenured instructors laughed and ate and chatted in full view of the many adjuncts on campus that afternoon. To us, they seemed only too pleased to rub our noses in our second-class status at the college. I decided to see for myself if we were being excluded on purpose, so I moseyed up to the spread of food and said, "Gee, it all looks so good."

The administrative assistant standing behind the table pointedly told me it was a "full-time instructors and staff" luncheon, looking all the while like she'd smack my hand if I dared even reach for a plate.

Now, I'm not one to push myself in where I'm not welcome, but, as they say out here in the west, it really "chapped my hide" to think that such a distinction would be so rigorously enforced between tenured and adjunct instructors. I realized then that I'd been laboring under the delusion that I was a valued member of the academic community on campus. That afternoon, I woke up and, while I wasn't permitted to do more than smell the coffee, I did become acutely aware of the status of adjuncts.

I began to notice that adjuncts, though we taught some fifty to sixty percent of all classes at the college, were viewed as somehow less qualified or less worthy. Even instructors with doctorate degrees from prestigious universities, who'd taught for years at Ivy League schools, were held in lower esteem once they became adjuncts at our college. This fact was not only reflected in the attitudes of many of the tenured instructors, but also in the abysmally low pay we received for each credit hour taught, and in a general lack of administrative support for our teaching efforts. Though the college received one of the highest reimbursements for full-time students (FTSE's) of the several community colleges in the state, adjuncts at the college were paid at a rate that put us close to the bottom in relation to the other colleges. We got no health insurance, retirement benefits, or preference in hiring when a full-time position opened. Adjuncts had no office where they could meet with students, no phone to use, and no room to sit down in for coffee breaks or lunch. I held many of my student conferences in the front seat of my vehicle.

While tenured faculty could use the copy machine in the administrative offices at any time (they each had a code number for the machine), adjuncts could not. By administrative decree, any photocopying that adjuncts needed had to be scheduled days in advance so it could be sent to the duplication department on the main campus. I taught classes in writing, and occasionally, I'd run across a poem or story that had relevance to my lesson for that evening, but unless I was willing to pay for copies at a copy shop, I knew I couldn't spontaneously run into the college office and get a dozen copies made right before class.

Tenured faculty had offices on campus and were usually assigned classrooms with locking closets so they didn't have to carry tons of books all over campus. Adjuncts got the rooms that were unoccupied for the moment and often had none of the maps or reference books provided the full-time faculty. The semester I taught basic writing, I twice requested a large dictionary for use in my class. No dictionary was ever provided.

When the adjuncts finally got an association going on both campuses, I volunteered for several committees, naively believing we might gain some measure of respect when the tenured faculty began to notice adjuncts at those meetings. I went to Faculty Senate meetings. I was the adjunct representative to Budget and Planning. A fellow adjunct attended the Learning Council, the new name for the President's Advisory Council. Other adjuncts attended the Strategic Planning and Assessment Committee meetings. Sometimes we were voting members and sometimes we weren't allowed to do anything but offer suggestions, but in each committee, we tried to find ways to bring adjunct concerns to the group in a positive manner. Beside the issues of low pay and no benefits, we had other items we thought needed to be addressed. We were excluded from filing for hearings by the Grievance Committee. We were excluded from participation in Staff Development Days that were held every semester. If we taught off campus (the college used classrooms in several nearby high schools), we didn't even merit a mailbox on campus.

For a time, things seemed to improve. We gained an invitation to attend a Staff Development Day. Of course, the president informed us, the college couldn't afford to feed lunch to the adjuncts, so the six of us who actually did attend took brown bag lunches rather than strain the budget. The president also pleaded a lack of seating space, so we carried folding lawn chairs to the meeting. A bus went to the main campus from our branch campus, but that was reserved for full-time faculty and staff. Though only three adjuncts from the branch campus wanted to give up a day to attend the meeting, there was no room for us on the half-empty bus, so we car-pooled to save gas. (Maybe it was better there was no room for us on the bus because it was evident they had issued the invitation in a grudging manner, and we would likely have found ourselves relegated to the back of the bus instead of being integrated into the ranks of the tenured instructors and full-time staff members.)

When the college hired a new president, many things changed drastically. Many of the former long-time employees were given their pink slips. Governance by decree from the office of the president was replaced with governance by committee. There were committees, committees, and more committees.

Each committee met and discussed and formulated in the belief that its ideas would be embraced. There was a general optimistic feeling that the dictatorial edicts of the former president had given way to a more democratic form for running the college. Shared governance by committee was the new president's theme.

Within the Faculty Senate, one tenured member and a couple of adjuncts took on the task of comparing and contrasting the several duties of full-time and adjunct instructors with an eye toward creating a more realistic job description for each. Adjuncts hoped that such a job description might be the first step toward the creation of a step-scale wage policy for adjuncts. After two years of work, the job descriptions were finally completed and forwarded to the office of the president for a signature. We heard nothing.

At the last meeting of the Faculty Senate right before the end of the spring semester, the president requested a few minutes to address the Senate. The president came with a list of suggested topics for the Senate to consider for the following fall semester. Can you guess what was on the list? JOB DESCRIPTIONS. Both the tenured faculty member and I strongly protested that we'd worked on job descriptions for two years, and our report was even then languishing on a desk in the president's office, awaiting only a signature of approval. At that, the president grew rather hostile and told us that education at the college level was in such a state of change that no one could foresee what the job of instructors would be in the near future, and that we should realize that what we'd worked on for two years would not adequately cover the instructor of the future. I thought we needed job descriptions for the present instructional staff, which could be modified in the future when the need arose, but my adjunct opinion carried no weight. Since I'm no longer an adjunct at the college, I don't know what was finally resolved about job descriptions, but I'd be willing to hazard a bet that no job descriptions exist for either tenured or adjunct instructors to this day.

That policy of asking committees to do the work, then ignoring the work of the committees seemed *de rigueur* for the new administration. After asking a committee to work up recommendations for some phase of the college's operations, the president often adopted a policy that bore little resemblance to what the committee had forwarded. The constitution that the adjuncts had been instructed to compose so we could be ratified as a viable association on campus had not been signed or ratified by the president either, and that document had been languishing on the president's desk for better than three years. Inquiries as to the status of our Adjunct Faculty Association or our constitution were met with silence. Letters asking about the fate of the constitution went unanswered. And through all of it, the tenured instructors, save for a very few, held themselves aloof from our struggles to achieve recognition and ratification, offering the excuse that their own constitution was also "in limbo."

While the president refused to recognize us as an association, the Compensation Committee was forced to acknowledge us when our adjunct association elected a computer accounting instructor as our representative to that committee. The accountant did his homework and could crunch numbers fast enough to challenge the assumptions of the tenured committee members. Nowhere was the tenured faculty's animosity toward adjuncts so evident as it was in that year's discussions about compensation once the accountant took up our adjunct cause. Sparks flew. Voices became shrill. It was a dogfight between the adjunct David and the tenured Goliath, and David's calculator was slinging numbers faster than Goliath could counter them.

While the president could find big bucks to send tenured faculty to Covey seminars (Stephen R. Covey wrote *The Seven Habits of Highly Effective People*), there didn't seem to be enough in the budget for the cost of living adjustment (COLA) that tenured faculty members vowed they needed to survive as residents of the city where the main campus was located. Why, the cost of houses and food and other necessities was just sky-high in that fair city, and they'd had minimal or no COLAs for several years. They didn't, however, believe that adjuncts merited any COLA at all, not even one percent. I guess that was because housing, food and other necessities cost adjuncts so much less than it cost the tenured instructors. Well, they reasoned, since we only worked part-time, our other source of income should be the one to provide us with a COLA. But our adjunct David prevailed, and we had the promise of a raise.

The tenured faculty membership was even more upset when adjuncts got a raise to $475 per credit hour, up from the $425 level where we'd started, while their COLA was held to two percent. The plan was to spread our $50 raise over two years, but even that was a point of heated discussion. One member of the Compensation Committee adamantly insisted that it be spread over three years, ranting that he needed a five percent COLA to catch up with escalating costs, and that if adjuncts got their raise over two years, he'd never get his COLA. He needed a five-percent increase in his base salary. I think he expected us to feel sorry for him and give up our $25-a-year raise so he could add an extra $2000 or more to his salary. Fat chance!

In the middle of salary discussions, I got a newsletter from a community college in Arizona. The president of the adjunct association in that metropolitan-area community college figured that he made something like $13,000 for teaching a tenured member's class load at his adjunct salary. He reasoned that the tenured instructor was making $40,000 for teaching the same classes, therefore, $27,000 of the tenured instructor's salary must be for duties other than instruction. He said he'd be willing to give up his adjunct teaching position (and the $13,000) to attend college committee meetings and other non-instructional functions if the state would pay him $27,000 for doing so. His humor was welcome at a time when the Compensation Committee was so full of rancor over salaries at our college.

While adjuncts were invited to sit on more committees, the attitude toward part-time instructors didn't change very noticeably. The President of the Faculty Senate, in a snit over not getting the COLA he thought tenured instructors deserved, stood up in the Learning Council and reiterated for the thousandth time the old saw that adjuncts "just wanted to teach their one class and go home." According to him, we had no further interest in the college. When the adjunct representative to the Learning Council came to our next Adjunct Faculty Association meeting and reported what the Faculty Senate president had said, I decided then that I had better things to do with my time. That was the last college committee meeting I went to. After attending meetings for three years, on my own time and at my own expense, the Senate president's statement was the last straw.

I don't understand, to this day, why adjuncts are thought to have a deleterious effect on education at the college level. Was my master's degree worth less because I was an adjunct instructor? I don't think so, but the tenured faculty seemed to believe that it was. Because we were paid less, we were judged to be worth less, which translated into "worthless" in many tenured instructors' minds.

Did my students get shortchanged because I was an adjunct instructor? I don't think so. I taught writing classes for four years. I'm also a working writer, so my knowledge not only comes from reading books, but also from writing them. I was always in class. I was always prepared. I was fair. My phone and mailbox numbers were available to every student I taught. The front seat of my vehicle was available for my published office hours. All my students' submissions were critiqued and back the following week, although I was holding down a full-time job and a second part-time job in addition to teaching.

Was I just interested in teaching my one class and going home? I don't think so. I was more often in attendance at committee meetings than the full-time instructors who were paid well to attend. I sometimes drove long distances to teach, and often drove considerable distances for meetings—sometimes attending two or three such meetings a week. Two hours at a college meeting in town and the half-hour drive before and after, and I'd lost three hours in income from my full-time job. Two hours at a meeting at the main campus and the drive there and back cost me four hours and thirty minutes in lost wages.

Am I still teaching my one class? I don't think so. As an "at-will" employee without benefit of tenure or a contract, I could be let go without so much as a "thank you" or an explanation. I was let go. Without a "thank you." Without an explanation. I didn't need one. All the most-involved adjuncts on our campus suffered a similar fate. All the committed and dedicated adjuncts who cared enough about teaching and the college to want to do more than "teach their one class and go home" are now *personae non grata* at the local community college.

We were once some of the college's most ardent supporters, but caring about adjunct conditions enough to speak out in favor of better treatment for adjuncts didn't win us any support from the college or from the tenured instructors in the end. Worse yet, the adjuncts we went to bat for, and who are still employed—the adjuncts who are now better paid because of our advocacy on their behalf—offered us no support when we were not rehired.

Do I still support the college? I don't think so. I taught there for four years and supported the college by teaching at one-fifth the salary they would have had to pay a full-time instructor. I think that's contribution and support enough.

Not invited to eat. Not invited to ride. Not invited to teach. Adjuncts, separate and unequal. South Africa has abandoned its policy of apartheid, but an academic apartheid still exists in the United States. At least it still exists on the small community college campus in the Southwest where I was once foolish enough to believe I was a contributing and respected member of the academic community.

Adjunct Misery

by Kathleen Joy Tigerman, Ph.D.

C all me an adjunct faculty, teaching academic staff or an ad hoc. Adjuncts carry forty percent of the teaching load at universities, yet are treated as second class citizens, denied the opportunity to teach upper division courses or identification by name in course schedules, refused monetary recognition of advanced degrees, given a tenth of the salary obtained by some colleagues, and denied insurance and retirement benefits. We are an exploited underclass in the educational caste system.

I won a teaching award from the students of a two-year institution where I ad hoced for five years but was denied a tenure track faculty position. Two years after I began working there, it became clear that two faculty positions would open. I discussed my prospects with the head administrator who was very encouraging, praising my work. He said that this was a teaching institution. The campus needed some new courses. He asserted that the development of a new course was equivalent to a publication. My colleagues were equally supportive, sharing their sense that I would get a faculty position. I developed four new courses. I got to teach summer school because there was a need for women's and minority literature—my specialties—and I "was cheap."

Apparently someone thought I was cheap in a different sense. I was propositioned by one of my supervisors, but in such a way that there was room for plausible deniability. I politely declined but received a negative performance evaluation from him.

Was this the reason I didn't get one of the two open faculty positions? It didn't help that I made a dumb move. I was assigned to teach a two-semester sequence of Masterpieces of World Literature. I asked the new chairman what he wanted for course content, specifically whether he wanted me to teach the masterpieces of Western Literature or the world. He replied with a laughing reference to "dead white men" and said he welcomed course content that would be closer to the course title.

When one of my students petitioned to get "diversity" credit for taking my course, the head administrator of my campus urged me to petition that the course "Masterpieces of World Literature" get departmental acceptance as a minority studies course. The English department faculty are spread around many institutions throughout the state, meeting only twice a year. My motion got long and heated debate at a meeting and was defeated. Unfortunately, this episode embarrassed the new chairman.

When I saw him next, a year or so later, he was chairing the hiring committee. There was no warmth in his manner toward me. All of the committee members were friends of mine; we had been colleagues for five years, and they were far better acquainted with my work than the chair who was rarely seen on our campus. The head administrator of my campus was a nonvoting member. In spite of the unanimous desire of the committee members to hire me, the chair would not permit it. He said that I had no publications, and that I had failed at demonstrating my teaching method.

I didn't understand why the courses I developed didn't count as publications, as my head administrator had asserted, but then, of course, discussion of some of those innovations made the chair look like a fool.

71

I died. From being creative and productive, I sank into a terrible depression, a place where, in varying degrees, I have spent most of my childhood and adulthood. Many times, through meditation and yoga, I have pulled myself out of the slough of despond, but this time I could not shake the pall enveloping me. I still had to finish out the semester, plus was scheduled to teach my favorite course, Voices of Diversity, during summer school.

This all comes back with such awful vividness. I was called to the head administrator's office. He asked if I would teach the summer school class. Yes. I asked him about what he had said about the development of a course being equivalent to a publication, and why he hadn't brought this up during the hiring committee meeting? He looked down, then suggested that I look at the situation not as a loss of a job, but as an opportunity for travel and adventure. I reminded him that I am a founding member of a nearby intentional community and deeply rooted in place. I have given exemplary service to this institution. He agreed and said he would write a glowing letter of recommendation.

About the chair's other assertion that I hadn't demonstrated my pedagogical method during the interview: I used a method that derives from Socrates and Paulo Freire. From Socrates, I borrowed the use of dialogue, and from Freire, the teacher's projection of equality between herself and students. If done well, this methodology is nearly invisible—except in its palpable empowerment of students. The students awarded me their teacher of the year award.

Of the two people hired when I was let go, one has left. My friends tell me this assistant professor did a prodigious amount of publishing—a novel and three articles in one year while teaching eight courses—and was hired away by a far more prestigious school. I hear on the grapevine that the other person is also a dedicated writer and on campus only for classes and office hours, unlike the full-time presence I had on campus when I was an ad hoc. So within a few years, there had to be another search, consuming the time of very busy and dedicated people, and the campus ethos of faculty presence in a family-like atmosphere is lessened. The campus, forced by the administration and their publish-or-perish dictum, has replaced two dedicated teachers with two dedicated writers.

My friends are the heroes of this story. After my dismissal, they reorganized the hiring procedures so that the campus would be empowered to hire, rather than have an open position controlled by a person who was unacquainted with campus needs. The year after I was "let go," a woman in another department faced a similar hiring fight. She had been told her performances did not count as publications, and she would not be promoted from ad hoc. But because of the faculty assertion of power and reorganized hiring procedures, she was hired to a faculty position.

What worked here? The faculty, at personal risk to themselves for doing it, made joint cause with the ad hocs, and won some justice from administrators more concerned with their own careers than with what was good for the campus and the people involved.

If this exemplary action were to occur on every campus, a united faculty could take back the power usurped by the administration's divide and conquer strategy. By doing this work of empowerment, we can inspire ourselves with this example of my former colleagues, and by the UPS workers, where full-timers struck over wages for part-timers. As a united faculty, we could reestablish teaching to its rightful place of power, and the faculty as the eloquent voice of the people.

Strange Fish

by John D. Nesbitt

I had been teaching English as a grad student for five years, part-time, when I received an appointment to teach a section of composition at a branch campus of a community college. I had done an internship at the same place a year before, which meant that I had worked for free, grading papers and giving lectures for the regular instructor. Now he was on sabbatical, and his workload was divided up among a few adjuncts, including me.

The course had been going along smoothly enough, I imagine. One day about halfway through the semester, I was answering questions about usage—specifically the difference between "lie" and "lay"—when a stranger walked into the room. He was carrying a large frozen fish, about two feet long, wrapped in a transparent plastic bag. He laid it on the desk of a student who was sitting in the front row. Then, after looking around at all the rest of us, he said to the student, "Now I want you to tell all of them what this is about." He took us in with a sweep of his arm. "I want you to tell them in good, proper English." And he left.

I have no idea what kind of an expression I had on my face, but I did have the presence of mind not to make any more of the incident. The student was a middle-aged woman, ten or fifteen years older than I was, and far and away the best student in the class. I could tell she was mortified. After class, she apologized to me and gave me an explanation.

She told me the man's name, which meant nothing to me. Then she went on to explain that he was a friend of her husband's. He had been telling her and her husband of his good luck catching sturgeon, and he had told her he would bring her some fish.

A few days later, to my surprise, I saw the man again. He was sitting behind a desk in one of the business offices of the college, where he seemed to be working normally at paper work. The incongruity astonished me. Up until that moment, I had assumed he was some sort of displaced person—one of those well-dressed, well-groomed people with a blown fuse—who didn't have much better to do than to go fishing and to wander into public institutions during business hours. Now I saw that he worked at the college but had apparently little regard for the educational process.

To be sure of his identity, I asked the student. She confirmed that he was the same person, and she told me his name again. It took me a while to absorb the whole idea. I knew the school where I was teaching was a pretty flaky place. The branch director had told us all, quite explicitly, that they didn't believe in the grades "F" or "D," and I had observed that my mentor (now on sabbatical) assigned very little work and graded none at all. I imagined that the man with the fish was acting within the bounds of normal behavior at that school.

Not long after that, I dropped by the sabbatical instructor's house to tell him how things were going in his absence. I narrated the incident with the fish, and I told him I was thinking of filing a formal complaint.

He told me that the fellow in question was just a big joker, who had pulled off similar antics with other people he knew. I shrugged and said it was fine if the fellow's pals thought he was funny, but he didn't know me and hadn't come to talk to me about it afterward either. What might be a gag to someone else was simply a professional offense to me, I said.

We talked a little while longer, and my senior colleague told me of other strange behaviors of professors on the main campus—faculty members who flagrantly did not show up for class, proclaimed their availability for homosexual experimentation, and so forth. I asked him why someone like that, who was obviously tired of his job, even bothered any more.

His faced widened as he said, in a semi-conspiratorial lowering of the voice, "You only have to work fifteen hours a week!"

That was his workload—fifteen class hours a week. By his reckoning, then, a person didn't have to prepare class, grade papers, hold office hours, work on curriculum development, or do other paper work.

This conversation gave me additional insight into the place where I was working. Apparently, people did not step on one another's toes, and everyone was left to go about his or her own business in his or her own peculiar way. Still, I told the sabbatical instructor that I was going to file a complaint if I didn't receive an apology.

The next week, the man from the business office approached me at school and told me he had heard I was thinking of filing a complaint.

I told him I had harbored such a thought.

Well, he assured me, there was no need for that. He and that lady were good friends, and it was just a little joke, that was all. Now that he thought of it, he realized he should have said something to me about it. He realized now that maybe he shouldn't have interrupted my class that way, but he wanted me to know he was just a practical joker, and he was always doing something like that.

We shook hands, and I assured him everything was all right. I really didn't think a formal complaint would do any good anyway. All I really wanted was an apology, and I got it.

But life has never been the same after that. I don't know how many times I have been asked to explain the difference between "lie" and "lay" since that day. Every time I have begun the explanation, I have remembered that incident. On some occasions, I have managed to give a straightforward explanation and suppress the memory. On other occasions, I have ventured into the absurd, with a comment such as "You can lay a frozen fish on the desk," and then, upon meeting the odd stares of the students, I have gone on to tell the story. But regardless of how I have handled the situation, I have always glanced at the door.

That incident took place twenty years ago and over a thousand miles away, but I imagine there are idiots like that man lurking in many of our hallways; and not all of them have just come in off the street.

The Witch and the Wimp

There's no doubt about it. Tension had been mounting ever since I confronted the newly designated department chair about her decision to replace me as thesis advisor. But on a calm Thursday in December when the dean designate of our about to be School of Public Health, a little guy with a moustache and round wire-frame glasses, called me into his office, I had no idea what was about to happen.

"Got a minute to talk?" he asked amiably when I arrived for my normal office hours.

"Sure," I said. I figured he was going to respond to the letter I had written, copied to him, asking the woman who hired me when she was struggling to build a track within the MPH Program, why she was now about to "dis" me, despite rave reviews from the dozens of students I have mentored through the successful completion of their graduate degrees.

Instead, fumbling with his tie and looking at his toes, he handed me a letter.

"At this point, I think the best approach is to announce to the students that you will be leaving as of January 1, and that we wish you well," it said.

Incredulous, I stared at him.

"Under the circumstances..." he mumbled.

"And what are those circumstances?" I asked. My contract was to run for another six months, and I was scheduled to begin teaching a core course in another month. My student evaluations had been excellent, my peer reviews superb, my performance steady and unquestionably good. He agreed with all this. "It's not performance related," he told me.

While he tried to think of an answer that would make any sense at all, the sign on his wall that said, "THE FUTURE SCHOOL OF PUBLIC HEALTH AND HEALTH SCIENCES" slid off its mounting and crashed to the floor.

"The ultimate metaphor," I said, rising to leave the room before the tears flowed. He found this absolutely hilarious and melted into uncontrolled giggling.

I couldn't resist one further question. "When you wake up in the morning and look in the mirror to shave," I asked, "what kind of man do you see there?" It is my fervent wish that for the rest of his life, every day of every week of every year, the man in the mirror will be tormented by this query.

How did we come to this juncture? How in nearly four years, had I fallen so far from grace in the eyes of the woman whose program I helped to build? And how had this man, who was her boss, failed his management responsibility so badly?

The immediate answer is The Letter. The one I wrote on hearing, incidentally from two colleagues, that I was being arbitrarily replaced as thesis advisor by a man (also an adjunct faculty) whose credentials for such a task were questionable at best, and whose past included some pretty interesting allegations relating to the topic of the day, namely sexual harassment. In The Letter, I dared to raise my concerns and my voice, I suppose, about the impact of this decision on the program, the sexism implicit in the move (without me as an active adjunct, there were no senior women in the program; even the support staff, I noted, were male) and the personal insult inherent in denying me this post. The Letter infuriated my colleague, if I may use that egalitarian term. She no doubt saw it as insubordination. The real issue was, of course, that I kept standing up to her in one way or another, refusing to be the quiet handmaiden she sought, the doer behind the scenes, quietly and without complaint and credit. This was a rather strange expectation on her part since we are of equal age and experience. In fact, I am slightly older and more experienced, but it was not surprising to those who know her character.

And character was central to what was going down here. Mine—full of fire when I have been wronged—fosters my unwillingness to fall quietly in step. Ever the crusader, and viscerally against invisibility and injustice, I am compelled (often with fatal results) to take a stand. Hers—European elite, coldly insecure, absolutely status struck, and very spoiled--renders her incapable of making sound decisions when they represent a threat to her authority and identity. And his? A wimp. A wet. A eunuch. Absolutely lacking in balls, to use the vernacular. The Queen's page. The only thing surprising here was not that he was such a poor manager, but that he was a man of so little character all together.

Prior to this crisis, my affiliation with the program had gone well, notwithstanding the angst the Queen and I caused each other. I enjoyed developing and delivering courses that the students call "cutting edge." It had been insightful to serve on the Admissions Committee, and advising students, while a formidable challenge in some cases, had had its own rewards. The teaching life was good, I thought. Along with writing and some consulting, it was where I want to be at this stage of my life and career. It gives meat, and meaning, to my professional persona.

And so, for days after the stunning blow was delivered, I wept. I grieved. I ranted. What is the point of performing well in the workplace, I asked my friends, rhetorically. Who will look after my students, with whom I had such solidarity. Who will teach my courses (so popular the students have petitioned to make them required)? How do the perpetrators of such injustice prevail?

The students wrote letters of protest. Some asked the school newspaper to cover the event. (They declined upon learning that my contract was to be bought out.) They called to cheer me up. The Associate Dean designate, who was left out of the loop entirely and who was furious at the "irrationality" and "professionally irresponsible behavior" of those responsible for my demise, sent me a great letter of recommendation. We talked.

"It's such a sad commentary on the program," I lamented.

"You're telling me?" he said. "And I still have to work here."

All of this helped. But none of it took away the sting. Because it was so blatantly unfair. Because I love teaching and am really good at it. Because I think mentoring young professionals is a privileged opportunity. Because I had to reinvent myself, yet again. Because "nice guys finish last." Because the Witch and the Wimp have gotten away with it, and none of us, least of all me, has been powerful enough to stop them.

My teaching friends tell me that my experience is not all that unique. "Academia is the worst," they say. "Cruel" and "political" keep cropping up as adjectives, as in "a cruel joke," or "a political move." "It's perverse and predictable," one veteran offered. Maybe. But I am not a tenure track, publish or perish professor. I'm just an adjunct trying to do my thing.

And that shouldn't sound like a fairy tale to me.

From the Shade of the Tower

by Kathleen Burk Henderson

Guerilla Professor. Bag Lady of Literature. I have described myself in a number of ways. I have been variously described as well; perhaps no more tellingly than Visiting Assistant Professor in an institution from which I earned two graduate degrees, and at which I taught, beginning eight years later, for four years, two part-time, two full-time. As in the board game, I was just visiting, and I was never allowed to forget it, although while visiting I was allowed to direct the undergraduate writing program for two years, organize and direct two interdisciplinary conferences that received national recognition: no less than the impact pages of *The Chronicle of Higher Education*. The department chair, whom I had known for over fifteen years when she hired me to teach, was clear: do not expect tenure; do not expect permanent employment; we will not tenure anyone else with an in-house Ph.D. This was amusing for there were a number of faculty members who had in-house degrees, that many more with in-house bachelor's degrees who had done graduate work elsewhere and returned. It is a Catholic school, only forty years old. Were it not for homegrown faculty, it would have no faculty at all. I was, it seemed, the point at which they were willing to draw the line. So, after four years, during which time two tenure track positions in my department were advertised and filled, I was dumped. I was warned, wasn't I? Why should I, how could I, be ungrateful?

Let me be clear: I am fully qualified. I earned the doctorate seventeen years ago, but in those seventeen years, I have been employed full-time teaching in my field for only four. Those four years were non-consecutive and non-tenure track. The rest of the time I was an adjunct at three institutions. I have published several articles, have a book manuscript nearly finished, have read papers at an international conference and at the famous MLA convention. Yet I am, at present, unemployed, and given recent experience, unemployable.

My first teaching assignment after defending the dissertation was indicative of the direction my career would take. I found a toehold at the small Liberal Arts College where I had been an undergraduate. When I visited the campus for the formal interview and offer process, a former professor, and when I was first a student, the only woman in the department, called me into her office to tell me that she had no objection to my being hired as a leave replacement, that she had nothing against me personally, but that she would see to it that I would not be hired permanently because I was an alumna of the place. I didn't believe her; I felt sure I would prevail, but she was as good as her word. Two years later, the morning after I delivered my third child, I was unemployed. They hired instead another woman who was on staff but not tenure track. She resigned after a year.

There were a number of protests of the decision to release me, including one by the president, but the department chair, now within a few years of retirement and weary of acrimonious interdepartmental battles, would not cross his colleague for me. I was dead meat. My family and I moved back to the city we had left years before.

I was not yet ready to despair. I had proven myself capable of good teaching; I still loved my subject. I would continue to try to accomplish the impossible, knowing that my commitment to remaining married to the father of my children, while the right moral and emotional choice, placed severe restrictions on my ability to climb the professional ladder. I knew from experience and from the grapevine that no institution in this major urban area was interested in hiring a Ph.D. from my program in my field. So when I received a call to teach as an adjunct at the local branch of the state university system, I jumped at it. I was not naïve: it was the best I could get under the circumstances, and I believed I could maneuver more easily from inside than from outside. Part-time teaching gave me time to look after my kids and time to teach. I was content for the moment. As adjunct positions go, I was fortunate: I taught only upper division students, juniors and seniors, I had complete autonomy in text selection and course description, and it paid better per course than any other place in town, save one. My education was still incomplete, however, since I still believed that being a part-time member of the faculty would give me an advantage in becoming a full-time member of the faculty. I was to learn otherwise.

The first semester I taught there, no enrollment cap was placed on my class. I ended up with more than sixty people on my roll. In a labor intensive subject like literature, with no teaching assistants (they are assigned to real teachers), this is deadly. I stood it only once, insisting that in the future the class be split; same work load, twice the money. They agreed, after I had proven myself capable of the job.

Almost immediately, I was called upon to step into a very awkward and delicate situation. A female professor in the department suddenly became very seriously ill, too ill to complete the term. The dean called me and asked if I would step in and take over this professor's classes at mid-term: an upper division class and a graduate seminar in my area of expertise. He offered me a flat fee, which was slightly more than what I would have received for teaching the two courses in their totality. It would be terribly difficult, I knew, but it would be my first opportunity to teach graduate students and teach in my field. I agreed. The professor asked that I accompany her to the last classes she would meet, in order to introduce me, explain the situation, and ease what everyone acknowledged was a complicated transition. She was gracious enough, under the circumstances, but she could not resist the impulse to test me in front of the students, asking me about a fairly obscure reference to Teilhard de Chardin, whose writings had influenced Flannery O'Connor. I never knew if she had been relieved or disappointed to learn that I knew a good deal about the question she had asked.

I finished the semester, during which I was also teaching a single course at a local community college. I proctored the final exam on the evening of my youngest child's second birthday; I missed the cake and ice cream. Having established by this time a reputation as a capable classroom performer, I was asked by the Director of the American Studies program to teach a summer course in the American Bestseller. A stretch, to be sure, but I believed that this confidence in me would lead to some more substantial recognition. That fall, a position opened in the department. Naturally, I applied for it. The professor whose place I had taken had recovered somewhat and was back on campus; in fact, she was the chair of the position search committee. I thought I was in, but when months went by with no word on my candidacy, I spoke to the dean. A few days later, the professor called me into her office to inform me that I would not be considered for the position because I did not have enough experience.

My inexperience did not stop them from continuing to ask me to teach anything that needed teaching. I was being taken advantage of; everyone knew it. For my part, I agreed to it because a little money is better than no money, and I was teaching substantive courses--Modern Period, Faulkner--rather than lower division surveys to good students. The health of my *skandalon* professor continued to deteriorate. She was scheduled to teach a graduate seminar in Faulkner the following fall but was by then too ill to begin the semester. In fact, she died shortly thereafter. I was again called upon at the last minute to step in for her. It necessitated introducing myself to the class on the first day so they would not call me by her name the whole term. I waited for the drop slips to come in, but only one did; in fact, one of the graduate students had been an undergraduate in the class, which I had taken over at mid-term before. Her obvious pleasure that I would be teaching the class was very gratifying and helped to reassure the others that all would be well. If I thought that I was in a fortuitous position to step into the vacancy this professor's death brought to the department, since I had assumed her identify more than once, I was again mistaken. They hired another person into a tenure track position to teach the courses I had been teaching. My request to be given permanent part-time status, or permanent full-time untenured status, was denied. Although I was repeatedly told how much they appreciated all I had done for them, how much they valued me as a colleague, it would be two years before I was asked to teach anything there again. Some of them wrote downright effusive letters of recommendation for my placement file, but awkward silences fell whenever I walked into the office. No one could look me in the eye. I was not their colleague; I was their dirty little secret. Their duplicitous treatment of me pricked their consciences, though not enough to do the right thing.

When I returned to the campus two years later, I would face the most harrowing experience of my professional life. Before I had even received my class roll, I received a confidential notification from Student Services concerning a student who had registered for the class. I had received similar notifications before of students with learning disabilities or physical disabilities so that suitable accommodations could be made. This was no problem. Nothing could have prepared me for a student who attempted to tyrannize my classroom and terrorize me. I was later to learn that he had already intimidated, indeed frightened, other members of the faculty and the administration, even threatening to sue for discrimination. The threat of a lawsuit against a university for violation of affirmative action guidelines makes administrators quake. Engendering such a response was apparently this student's primary objective. He may have been serious about acquiring a college degree; he certainly was not serious about learning anything anyone might be able to teach him, convinced as he was, that he already knew everything. The details of my dealings with him are a story for another day. It suffices to say that since I was merely an adjunct teaching a required course, he expected to run roughshod over my classroom and me. He did not know that I had been insulted by experts; I am not easily bullied.

But I am not stupid either. Bereft of all else, I still clung to my professional integrity. I was very careful with him, but it wasn't enough. He filed a complaint against me with the Civil Rights Commission. When this became known to the administration, I was called into several very anxiety-laden meetings with the College Master and the Vice President of Academic Affairs. I was assured that I would have the full support of the university should any litigation be instigated. I thanked the vice president for saying so, but begged to be forgiven if I remained dubious. Threatened with another legal action by this savvy and exploitative student, who obviously knew the ins and outs of the bureaucratic labyrinth, I believed that I, as an adjunct, would be hung out to dry by a nervous administration desperate to minimize their liability and responsibility.

In the frantic time between the end of fall term and Christmas, a representative of the Civil Rights Commission was dispatched from Washington to investigate the charges leveled against me. I was unable to meet with her personally, but she interviewed me in a lengthy telephone conversation. By the time our conversation was concluded, the official indicated that she was irritated to learn she had been sent on a wild goose chase, wasting her, my and the government's time and money. The student's charges were completely bogus. I heard nothing more about the matter, but the fact remains that I had been placed in an extremely vulnerable position, and frankly, I didn't get paid enough to subject my family and myself to that kind of stress.

Meanwhile, in what seemed at the time a fortuitous, if not providential, development, the other institution from which I had received my degree years before, and where I had also been teaching as a part-time adjunct, offered me a full-time, but non-tenure track contract for the next year. I took it, greatly to be relived to be out of the adjunct rat race, receiving a salary, which a little more closely approached what I was worth, and hoping it would lead, at last, to permanent employment.

There were advantages to teaching at the place where I had gone to graduate school, although I had not really aspired to it. I loved the curriculum, which was standardized for the first four semesters, and my students, though mostly freshmen, were good, averaging as an entering class, just less than 1200 on the

SAT. There were, I knew well, worse places to teach. For the two years I was part-time, I "squatted" in the office of a former professor, who spent very little time on campus. My classes were all in the morning; he arrived in the afternoon, so our paths did not cross. I was still just visiting, however; I had not a drawer or shelf to call my own. While looking for such a drawer in his obviously unused desk, I found a set of student themes that were twenty years old, but mine went home in my bag with me every day.

When I was given a full-time contract the next year, I was allowed to occupy the empty office of a professor whose one-year leave had been extended for another year. He was very gracious, clearing a bookshelf for me and having a small file cabinet moved in. Here was my chance to make a place for myself, to make an identity of my own, to come out of the shadows and be seen for myself. I was released from teaching one regular course in exchange for directing a much-troubled undergraduate writing assistance program. There was no agreement on the status of the program: The English Department chair and the associate provost strongly supported it; the provost was at best indifferent; at worst, hostile to its existence since it acknowledged what he desperately wished not to acknowledge: that there were students at his university who could not write. His ostrich-like strategy for redressing the situation was to recruit better students, like those at MIT, where his brother is tenured. Knowing all these people as I did, being grudgingly allotted the scantest of resources, and having realistic expectations for the enterprise, I did a good job of carving a niche for the Writing Program. I also developed and implemented a summer program for incoming freshmen to help them get a head start on the writing task ahead of them. In the meantime, a search was conducted to fill a position in the department. When I formally applied for it, I was reminded that I could not be considered because I had an in-house Ph.D.

In an eerie *déjà vu* experience, the end of my first-full-time year brought the death of the professor in whose office I had lived as a ghost. He had a heart attack while attending an out-of-town conference. As before, I was asked to occupy the place he vacated in the department and was extended a second one-year contract. I continued to direct the Writing Program, teach the summer program, teach the regular courses, and, on my own initiative, I organized two interdisciplinary conferences that consisted of lectures and presentations centering on issues raised by plays produced by the Drama Department. I did all this for a salary a third lower than that of the person who was hired into the position I had been denied, fresh out of graduate school in his first job. I even had to show him where his classroom was on his first day; it was adjacent to mine. Because of the unexpected vacancy caused by the senior professor's death, another tenure track position was written into the budget. Again, I applied for it, thinking that all the work I had done for the university would not go unrewarded. This time, in a sublimely ironic twist, my application was formally, that is to say technically, considered before being rejected. My suspicions as to why this bit of legerdemain took place were soon confirmed. Another member of the faculty, like me an in-house Ph.D. and non-tenure track, but unlike me, of the same gender, academic discipline, and political persuasion as the provost, was also applying for a position in the Politics Department. He got the job. I got taken to lunch. The formal letter of rejection was signed by the acting chair of the department, an in-house Ph.D.

Some may think that the mistreatment of non-tenured faculty is a phenomenon of the overgrown state university systems. It is pervasive and pernicious. When it occurs in small private institutions, the sting is sharper. Because they have the latitude and discretion to act on a situational basis, it is obvious the rejection is personal and arbitrary. There is no anonymous, bureaucratic, institutional policy behind which pusillanimous acts may be veiled. The polished ivory tower houses the same pettiness, jealousy and vindictiveness as the drab, utilitarian, industrial megaversity fortress. And the dungeon, though smaller, is deeper.

Farewell to Matyora*

by Anesa Miller

A s an idealistic young adult in the mid 1970s, I was keen to find a meaningful application for my talents—something that would let me indulge my penchant for the exotic yet also be of use to society. In high school, I had done well in foreign languages, and the history and culture of our then archenemy, the Soviet Union, captured my interest when I read *The Brothers Karamazov* during my freshman year of college. In 1979, when I stood before my first Russian-language classroom, as a graduate student at the University of Kansas, I believed I had found my calling. What could be more worthwhile than teaching Americans to speak Russian, to communicate with our nation's foe, forging the links of a grassroots diplomacy that would eventually pull official discourse in a peaceable direction? This seemed to be a mission worthy of all my youthful energies.

I worked in my chosen profession for fifteen years, including the time it took to complete my dissertation while raising

*With Apologies to Valentin Rasputin

two children. Over that period, I received many awards, published articles and translations, edited books and garnered consistently positive student evaluations. In testament to the impracticality of a permissive upbringing, such matters as salary and benefits were not my major concerns. I accepted the fact that my income as a part-time instructor was even less than what I'd earned as a graduate teaching assistant. Waiting for the full-time opportunity to come along, I subsisted on a combination of loans, multiple jobs and help from relatives.

But about five years ago, I finally concluded that it was time to choose a new career. The enthusiasm that led a Midwestern girl to reach out to an unknown nation and master its language is now a thing of the past, and the idealism that pushed financial worries to the back of my mind has given way to despair that my own educational debt now limits the help I can offer my children as they approach college age.

Circumstances at my last place of employment fell heavily on the camel's back of my dedication to teaching and scholarship. From 1986 through 1994, I was employed in the Department of Modern Languages (DML) at a public university that I'll call by the fictitious acronym SUO. There I encountered a level of deceit and pettiness that led to my disillusionment with the industry of higher education. Attempts to find satisfaction, first through internal grievance procedures and then the Equal Employment Opportunity Commission, proved to be a lengthy exercise in futility.

Things hadn't always looked so bleak. In the fall semester of 1993, shortly after I completed my Ph.D. (with honors), the DML opened a full-time instructorship in my field. Two senior faculty members mentioned that they hoped the new position would soon be up-graded. Our acting chair—a woman I will call Dr. Naphta (with apologies to Thomas Mann, author of *The Magic Mountain*)—said she had asked the dean to make it a tenure track position; supposedly her request came too late for the next academic year, but she felt certain that the dean understood "our staffing needs." Dr. Volodin (with apologies to Alexander Solzhenitsyn, author of *The First Circle*), DML's only full-time professor of Russian and co-chair of the hiring committee, assured me that he had a written guarantee from the College of Arts and Sciences that an assistant professorship in Russian would be approved within the coming year. I applied for the job with these high hopes in mind.

It was early February when a secretary with whom I was friendly mentioned that she had made arrangements for three job candidates to visit campus for interviews over the coming week. Since my application for the job had not even been acknowledged by that time, I began to worry that I hadn't made the short list, and so I dropped Dr. Naphta a note asking her to confirm that my credentials had been received. Within a few days, she contacted me to arrange an interview. She also told me to make an appointment with the Dean of Arts and Sciences as part of the process. These meetings took place within the next several days and seemed to go very well from my naïve perspective.

Although another week went by without an announcement of the committee's decision, I was no longer afraid of being passed over. I had learned that only one of the three outside candidates had a Ph.D. in hand, and none had my years of teaching experience. It seemed that I was the best qualified and very well might get the offer.

The following Tuesday, Dr. Naphta asked me to come by her office for a private meeting. She said that Dr. Volodin would join us, the two of them having formed a subcommittee to address certain "special concerns."

Once the office door closed, Dr. Naphta announced that she had called me in to discuss several instances of "unprofessional conduct" on my part. She said that these "strikes against" my job candidacy had undermined the committee's decision-making process and placed her, personally, in an awkward and unpleasant position.

Tall and austere, with close-cropped, steel gray hair, Dr. Naphta was an unmarried woman some fifteen years my senior. Relations between us had previously been cordial, but at this meeting, her tone was stern yet condescending. I was shocked by the charges she enumerated.

First, she claimed that I had falsified the rank of my current position on the vita submitted with my application, presenting myself as an assistant professor rather than an instructor. "And a *part-time instructor*, at that," as she put it. In actuality, I had received the rank of assistant professor when I finished my Ph.D. the previous spring. Sadly, this entailed no material improvements since my appointment remained part-time. The *pro forma* promotion was conferred by the university Contracts Office without input from DML, and Dr. Naphta was evidently unaware of it.

I offered to fetch documentation from my office, but as fate would have it, my contract was nowhere to be found. Instead, I grabbed a list of departmental telephone numbers that included the abbreviation "Asst. Prof." beside my name. Dr. Naphta scoffed at this as proof of anything other than secretarial error.

In the heat of the moment, I didn't think to suggest that Dr. Naphta locate the copy of my contract that must have been on file in her own office. Nor did I ask her why an apparent problem with my credentials hadn't been brought up sooner, when I first submitted them more than two months before. At the time, it seemed best for me to say as little as possible because I quickly became so upset, I was afraid of blurting out some angry remark that might make matters worse.

Dr. Naphta then moved on to "Strike two." It seemed that I had conducted myself unprofessionally at my interview some ten days before. Specifically, I had insisted on asking questions "in an inappropriate manner," rather than simply describing my qualifications, as would befit a job applicant. Supposedly, the dean had called to tell Dr. Naphta that he was seriously displeased with my behavior.

I had to confess that I did, in fact, pose the questions she listed, namely: whether it might be possible to up-grade the instructorship to a tenure track position and, after receiving a negative answer, when an opening at the assistant professor level might be expected. I pointed out to Dr. Naphta that questions about opportunity for advancement could hardly be inappropriate at a job interview, but she replied ominously that it was not my place to "question the rank of the position."

This seemed perplexing, as she herself had once voiced disappointment with the dean's reported decision to hold off on opening a tenure track. I was also surprised that Dr. Volodin offered no comment on this, since he had led me to expect an opening at the higher rank no later than the next academic year.

Then came the third and most serious strike against me: my husband of two years, a senior professor in the Biology Department, had attempted to interfere in DML affairs by mentioning to the dean that if I moved to take a job elsewhere, he too would probably relocate. The dean had seen fit to repeat these statements to Dr. Naphta, who claimed that, "The administration is very angry about your husband's threats. He has put us in an awkward position, indeed."

I made another brief attempt to justify myself, pointing out that my husband had not meddled in DML affairs—it seemed the dean had done that himself by passing the remarks on to Dr. Naphta. Again, she brushed my protest aside.

Finally, Dr. Volodin struck a conciliatory tone, saying that he realized I might not have *asked* my husband to interfere, but I had to recognize that the committee was now faced with "an appearance of bowing to outside influence" if they offered me the position. The only solution was for me to apologize and promise that I "would not take recourse to improper channels of communication at any future time while employed in the department." Since this was clearly a condition for receiving the job offer, I swallowed my pride and agreed.

Appearing fully mollified, Dr. Naphta then said she would like to protect me from ill will that other members of the hiring committee were likely to bear toward me. For that reason, she wanted all three of us to pledge to keep the content of our meeting confidential. When I agreed to this as well, she said that a final vote of the hiring committee would take place the following day.

I have never been able to learn what the Dean of Arts and Sciences really said that placed Dr. Naphta in such an "awkward position." Some of my former colleagues have suggested that he may have reprimanded her for excess expenditures on a minor job search—travel to the Modern Language Association Convention to screen applicants and hosting three candidates on campus—when the best qualified turned out to be an insider who had already worked in the department for eight years. In that case, she may have wanted to vent her embarrassment on me.

Another possibility involves the stand my husband took in a unionization drive held earlier that academic year; he was the only Distinguished Research Professor to openly advocate joining the union, while most other titled faculty members came out against it. After such "disloyalty," the dean might have given Dr. Naphta cause to reprimand me in retribution, although he later denied this.

Whatever the true motivation behind them, Dr. Naphta's charges left me confused and discouraged. Two days after the confidential meeting, however, she paused while passing in the hallway to tell me that we must "put all that behind us and learn to work together." She said that the hiring committee had selected me, and an official offer would be forthcoming from the dean's office. Since so much time had already been lost, I should be prepared to reply promptly.

More than ten days passed before I had any further word on the position. Finally, an envelope arrived at my home by local mail that contained a completed contract. Every line, including rank and salary, had been filled in, leaving blank only the spaces for my signature and Dr. Naphta's. There was no accompanying letter of any kind.

I had assumed that an "offer" would entail the opportunity to negotiate certain job conditions. Resigned to the fact that an up-grade to a track position was out of the question, I had nonetheless arrived at the notion that the rank of *visiting* assistant professor might provide something for everyone: it would spare me from taking a demotion without obligating the university to any greater commitment than the instructorship. Despite the "take-it-or-leave-it" appearance of the proffered contract, I decided to request that, in recognition of my previous rank and years of service, I be appointed as visiting assistant professor.

Over the course of the next week, I began to contemplate rejecting the job altogether if my request could not be met. One reason for this extreme decision was the frustration of turning from one office to the next as I tried to figure out who was ultimately responsible for negotiating the terms of contracts. At every level, I got a different answer. Dr. Naphta claimed that I couldn't be a visiting professor unless I was affiliated with some other institution—literally "visiting" from somewhere. She expressed doubt that the college would make an exception in my case but said that I was free to pursue my request if I insisted.

The Dean of Arts and Sciences discounted Dr. Naphta's argument. He said the Vice President for Academic Affairs had determined that an instructorship was the best "job line" for the Russian program at the current time. The vice president conceded that she had the authority to accommodate candidates' special needs, but that affirmative action considerations might make it impossible to do so in this case.

The Director of Affirmative Action said that he sympathized with my position and "would be willing to work with the department" if it chose to make a request on my behalf. In the absence of initiative at the departmental level, however, he was powerless to intervene. So returning to the start of the vicious circle, I realized that only Dr. Naphta could shepherd my request through the system, but she obviously would not consider undertaking such a favor on my behalf.

In my last weeks at SUO, when it became clear that each administrator I met with preferred to pass on my queries, I wrote a final letter to Drs. Naphta and Volodin, explaining my reasons for turning down the job at the rank offered: Being an instructor would not only appear as a demotion on my vita, it disqualified me from opportunities that could have significantly benefited my career advancement, such as grants from national organizations that fund research abroad. I still cherished hopes that Dr. Volodin might advocate for me at the eleventh hour, but a private conversation a few days later showed that my optimism was misplaced.

Dr. Volodin was convinced that the best way to solve staffing problems in the Russian program was by cooperating with the DML Chair to present a united front to the higher administration. He still believed that a tenure track position would be opened within one or two years, *if* the entire Russian faculty demonstrated the proper spirit of cooperation. He was surprised when I told him that the Dean of Arts and Sciences had inadvertently revealed quite a different scenario.

When I visited the dean, at the time he passed my attempt to negotiate rank on to the Vice President for Academic Affairs, I mentioned that senior faculty had encouraged me to believe a tenure track position would be opened very soon. He confirmed this—because the German program would need to replace a number of upcoming retirements. "That's good news for you," he suggested. "You'll be on the inside track."

"But I teach Russian," I explained. Like many people unfamiliar with the foreign-language professions, the dean assumed that an "instructor of modern languages" should be prepared to teach them all.

He covered his faux pas by extolling the security I would enjoy under the instructorship. After all, it was a five-year renewable position. That is, DML was assured of its renewal for five years; the individual instructor would only be contracted for one year at a time and could be replaced at the department's discretion.

This made clear to me why Dr. Naphta was touchy about the issue of up-grading ranks: she was determined to reserve tenure track positions for the German program, while maintaining the veneer of equality and collegiality among various programs. In fact, the paper trail that I was to follow a few weeks later showed that she never requested a track opening in Russian as she once claimed. A small department like DML stood little chance of seeing multiple professorships approved within a few-years period, so she had to lock the Russians into an ongoing instructorship. Otherwise the German faculty would have to give up their regular junkets to supervise students at the University of Salzburg and stay at SUO to staff courses instead.

When I explained this to Dr. Volodin, he seemed taken aback but, to the best of my knowledge, never protested Dr. Naphta's maneuvers. Nor did SUO's internal grievance committee find any validity in my complaint that DML denied my right to due process in hiring and negotiations. It might have turned out differently if the grievance committee had actually questioned the main parties, but Dr. Naphta departed for a year abroad in Salzburg before the committee's first meeting, and the dean, who had developed health problems, was never asked to respond.

It fell to mild-mannered Dr. Volodin to answer all of my charges. Based on his version of events, the committee concluded that DML did seem to have communication problems but nothing that warranted official chastisement or an apology to me.

I remained convinced that an objective authority would recognize the injustice of my situation, so I took my case to the State Equal Employment Opportunity Commission. Here the primary charge was discrimination on the basis of national origin because DML had routinely appointed adjunct faculty from China and the USSR at even higher ranks than the one I requested. (This issue was also included in my internal grievance but was dismissed on the recommendation of the Director of Affirmative Action, who evidently forgot his earlier "sympathy for my position.")

Documents that I obtained from the Contracts Office under the Freedom of Information Act revealed that DML's appointments of foreign nationals constituted a double standard in violation of the University Charter. No United States citizen had ever held a visiting professorship in DML, but during the years when I was employed there, three foreign faculty members served as visiting associate professors. Two of them held no academic degree beyond an M.A. (conferred by SUO itself). Nor did their transcripts show any prior experience or training in foreign-language pedagogy, contrary to the Charter requirement that "an associate professor must hold the Ph.D. or its equivalent and show evidence of significant scholarly activity" in the field of expertise that he or she is contracted to teach.

This situation is actually quite common. These faculty members were teaching their native languages while pursuing graduate studies in English and American Literature. Judging by their students' level of satisfaction, they were competent teachers, but judging by their credentials and official university criteria, they were not qualified to be associate professors. Certainly no more than I was to be an assistant professor. DML repeatedly showed favoritism by making exceptions in their rank appointments, while refusing to do as much for me.

The Director of Affirmative Action defended the practice by claiming that the terms of international agreements obligated the host university to recognize visitors' home ranks. However, protocols on file in the College Office contained no such stipulation, and in one case, the visiting associate professor was not even a participant in any exchange program.

Of course, it's no mystery why the DML favored foreign employees. On paper, SUO maintained a policy against placing "service obligations" on part-time faculty, but in fact, we were routinely asked to perform extra tasks. When I cooked Russian meals for student events, assisted with competency testing or directed a Russian choir, I was acting as a volunteer. In my final years on the job, however, I began to insist on payment for time-consuming services, such as simultaneous interpretation for the university president. By contrast, foreign faculty members never quibbled about rendering "service to the institution."

I know from conversations with these colleagues—with whom I was always on good terms—that they often did not realize translating documents for administrators or participating in German program events were not required duties. Those who did recognize these favors as an imposition on their time nonetheless felt they could not refuse. After all, foreign visitors who hope to remain in the United States permanently, or who simply don't want to jeopardize their prospects for one more year of wages in hard currency, feel vulnerable to the whims of their employers.

To my dismay, none of these issues impressed the EEOC. It declined to even consider my allegation of an eight-year pattern of discrimination, since those events fell outside the statute of limitations—six months prior to my filing date. As for the unfair reprimands and restriction of my freedom of speech, the Commission ruled that I had failed to prove they were committed with an intent to discriminate.

Since that time, college enrollments in Russian nationwide have declined by half, making it unlikely that I could ever return to teaching in my field. Students who were traditionally drawn to the language—political science majors, historians, members of ROTC and the occasional musician or nonconformist—now find more compelling interests elsewhere. Although such trends result from broad socio-economic pressures, I believe our universities bear some responsibility for turning students away. Students are deterred from taking on a meaningful challenge when academic advisors tell them to avoid "difficult" languages that might drain time from a job track program. And they are turned away when universities fail to support the kind of intellectual idealism that lets a young person believe communication—especially with one's supposed enemies—is still an essential mission in this world. As for me, I miss my students since leaving the profession, but nothing else about the academic life calls me back.

Two Years, One Quarter

by Peggy de Broux

In 1993, I was delighted to land an adjunct English position in a small city on Washington's peninsula where I had just purchased a home for my mother and me. I left Seattle and a full-time secretarial job to live there because it was time for me to take care of my mother, and my daughter already lived there and would be able to help with her. I was delighted to be in academia again after an eight-year absence.

The one English class a quarter I taught for seven quarters was about right, financially, to augment my mother's teacher retirement from Texas, where she had taught for fifty years in public schools. I feel very much at home on campuses and got into the swing, I thought, of this two-year college in a gorgeous setting: clear skies (when it wasn't raining), firs and spruce, bright spring flowers in April, warm weather in summer when there was little rain. It seemed ideal.

Two years later, I was asked to represent part-time teachers in the union. There were eleven at the time in the English Department alone, and there were well over one hundred part-timers working in the college because the school where I worked had the main campus as well as a number of satellite locations, including a program in a state prison.

Seldom did any of the outlying adjuncts attend faculty or union meetings, so it was a bit hard to actually "represent them" on the contract negotiation committee, which I attended during a spring and summer quarter. I was not teaching during the summer, and therefore was given no compensation for my involvement in the summer. We concluded negotiations during the fall quarter, in late November. This was my seventh quarter teaching English. I had taught conversational French a couple of quarters for the Continuing Education Division, but the school kept this to a two to three hour course, and the credits would not transfer to a college as language credits, so it seldom "made."

Also during the winter quarter, a new chairperson took over in the English department. She proceeded to divide the wheat from the chaff. Part-timers were NOT to participate in English Division meetings (as they had been doing the two years I had been there and long before). They were to have their own separate meeting with the chair, who would "report our concerns" to the rest of the English faculty.

Here is where things started happening. I led a revolt, with a few other part-timers standing behind me, some who had been with the school almost ten years. I photocopied an article from the union newspaper that dealt with part-time teaching across the nation, showing that many people had to hold down two and three jobs to keep going, with no benefits of any kind, usually. I asked the chair's permission to disseminate this material at our first "segregated" meeting. She did not object then, but she stood firm in her decision to keep us apart from the full-time faculty, despite the fact that we taught English 111 and 112, the basic courses which the regular faculty taught, in addition to their literature courses. Her argument was that ours were not the concerns of full-time faculty and couldn't be expected to be. This, in spite of the fact that I, for one, had not only been drafted to the salary negotiation committee, I was also on two other committees, and served, with a former English chair, as co-sponsor of gays and lesbians in the International Club. That might have been the problem right there: I learned from students that several faculty had already refused to sponsor them. In the classroom, I was determined to offer my English students diverse essays written by gays, blacks, Native Americans, Italians, all kinds of people.

Our chair unfairly said to us, "You didn't have to elect me chair," which was hilarious, as we had been segregated, the previous year, from just such a vote. We had no CHANCE to vote for or against her, of which I reminded her in the meeting.

That was probably the one-time-too-many that I opened my mouth. At the end of the quarter, December 15, 1995, I tried to find out if my books had been ordered for the spring, only to be told in a very backward manner, that I had no class for January. This was not the way adjuncts had been treated in the past. I had always been approached about a month before the end of the quarter to turn in a book order and was told which section I would probably teach. The dean, now a highly paid Vice President of Educational Affairs, who was previously Continuing Education Dean with no prior experience that I know of to qualify him for the job, told me verbally that they did not need me in January. When I asked him pointedly why, he suggested I talk to the Chair of the Division. When I finally was able to talk to her, personally, she said, "You'll have to talk to the vice president." I requested knowing what I was doing wrong, or what I could do to improve. I mentioned course evaluations from students. She could not have seen them prior to making this decision, as I did not get my copy for several months (long after I was gone from the campus). She admitted she had not read them and offered to do so. Nothing changed.

I was devastated! Personally! Having contributed extra time to committees and the annual Christmas program, (I was asked to read a French carol in the language, then its translation), I can only think that a part-timer should go to class, teach, never talk to students, never participate in the governance of one's college. That was the message the chair gave us that quarter. She seemed to favor certain adjuncts over others, without stating the criteria which she had used (there WAS NO WRITTEN CRITERIA for choosing adjuncts). Salaries for adjuncts were exactly the same for everyone, whether they had Ph.D.'s or M.A.'s (I had the latter in Comparative Literature), so one could not assume that the school wanted to hire inexperienced, lesser qualified people so they would have to pay less (which might have been the case in the full-time arena). One of my colleagues has a UC Berkeley Ph.D., was the wife of a tenured English professor, and was very seldom hired, though she and her husband made it clear that she desired adjunct teaching.

When there were real openings (two-full time positions were approved), many of the adjuncts applied, as did I, and only two were interviewed, along with two out of state candidates. One of those, formerly an adjunct, was awarded a full time position. She had been at the college one quarter less than I as an adjunct.

One other colleague, who had been teaching the English core courses for six or seven years, was never used again, following this new chairperson's taking the lead.

In addition, I had been rewarded as faculty by having my registration paid to the state Community and Technical College Conferences for two years in a row. The second year, I was part of the program and made a lecture/slide presentation about the NEA. In addition, the summer before I was no longer needed in December, the college awarded me $150.00 to attend a Writers' Conference. That same year, the Conference itself awarded me another $150 as a Naomi Clark Scholar. I cannot understand the College's finding a person worthy of such honors one year, only to let them go a few months later, replacing them with less seasoned part-timers. (They had also hired a retired Ph.D. as an adjunct in September, and he kept his position; he teaches two courses frequently and apparently does not want to work full time again.)

I wanted very much to sue, to report the College to the Human Rights Commission, to do something to let other people know I felt I had been discriminated against. On what basis? I'll never know whether it was ageism (I am now 62, an age when it is extremely difficult for me to get ANY kind of employment), their dislike of my choice to teach diverse materials to a small community college student body, or did I just raise too many questions? I waffled on going to the Human Rights people and was advised by my own family that I should consider how small the town is, and what my suit might accomplish, if anything. I was still on the Continuing Ed faculty. It was such an ordeal that I hated going on the campus for months. I finally did, as the French course had enough enrollment in the spring quarter, and I worked well with the Continuing Ed director, who seemed to have a heart but not much clout. He has repeatedly asked the administration why they do not offer a five-credit transfer French course. They offered Spanish and German, despite the fact that all the area high schools also teach French. I now have a three, rather than a two-hour French class: an hour and a half twice a week, which is my choice. That is my sole teaching responsibility now for this college.

I can't see the vice president or the former chairperson without a twinge of hate (which I don't like to feel for anyone). The president of the college took no interest in this type of problem. I knew I could not call upon him for help. There WAS no authority to whom I could appeal and get some kind of hearing, once I declined to go through the state's Human Rights Commission.

One thing has happened since: the college has reduced the ratio of full-time to part-time faculty, enabled by the fact that they now use part-timers to teach more than one class (when three classes is a full load, per quarter)? Another thing happened: the last quarter I was teaching, the adjuncts were FINALLY given an adjunct office, with a couple of telephones, three desks. I had to share an office, prior to this, and many of the part-timers had no office at all. I worked hard to get that office set up, in the committee, and got to enjoy it for one quarter only. What repayment.

Circles

by Brigitte Dulac

From the junk mail that my husband Dan and I would discard, the return address of an envelope protruded. It was from the Community College District. I pulled the envelope out. My address showed through the plastic window. I wrote it two weeks ago, applying for the full-time position at the college where I'd taught as an adjunct faculty for the past thirteen years.

The knife that I used to open the envelope nicked a corner of the enclosed form letter, the very half sheet of paper where, as requested, I had written my own address. Next to "THE FULL TIME POSITION FOR WHICH YOU APPLIED HAS BEEN FILLED," June 23 was stamped in bold print.

I turned the paper around, looked inside the envelope. There was no note from anyone at the district or at the college where I had taught all the French classes, from first semester beginners to the more advanced courses. I was still scheduled to teach in the fall as a part-time instructor.

I flung the form letter on the counter with the other junk mail. On the telephone wires above the wall, their bodies as tapered as bullets, blackbirds crowded one by one. "THE POSITION FOR WHICH YOU APPLIED..." I had expected the position as the best-qualified teacher available. I was in my fifties. I would never again have as good a chance for a full-time job.

Our cat, Minouche, her tail swishing like a hurried pendulum, watched the birds from behind the screen door. I retrieved the district letter from the rest of the mail. "...FOR WHICH YOU APPLIED HAS BEEN FILLED EFFECTIVE..." As if of one mind, the blackbirds on the wires dove into our yard. "...JUNE 23."

I crumpled the letter, hurled it at the window. It fell on the floor, and Minouche, forgetting the birds, batted it across the kitchen floor as if taking part in a game. She cuffed it under the refrigerator.

June 23 was the same date as Odette, the full-time instructor at the college, had told me she would leave for France. It had been after the interview as we perfunctorily kissed good-bye.

"I won't see you until next spring," she had said.

"When are you leaving?" I asked, surprised. If...when I got the job, wouldn't she want to tell me? See me to apprise me of her duties, her current priorities? She had, one year ago, when she had asked me to take over her job on a voluntary basis during her sabbatical leave.

"On the 23rd."

"Of June?"

"My whole family is coming with me. We'll spend one month in France before I meet with the Study in Paris students."

One month before meeting the students? Wouldn't that be July, not June? The dates did not seem to add up as if she were trying to avoid me. Too many things, however, whirled through my mind...the interviewing committee's warm greeting...the distant parting. I sensed that a break had occurred, a not too subtle shift in attitudes as if the committee's members too had been of one mind when, in turn, they repeated, "And what else do you do using this method? And what else do you do using this method?" Until I ran out of answers and examples.

It was because of Odette's semester in Paris that a full-time instructor had been needed to replace her. "THE POSITION..." I reached for the phone, dialed the Communications/ Foreign Language office at the college.

"Hi, Carol. This is Brigitte Dulac. Who's to fill the full-time position in French?"

"Raquelle Requin."

"Raqu...? But...!"

"What?"

"Thanks, Carol."

Raquelle was the daughter of Odette's best friend in France. She was not yet thirty, had just obtained her master's degree and had taught one summer for the district and one semester part-time at the college.

I hung up the receiver and immediately pressed the re-dial button. "Brigitte again. Is Terri in?" Terri was the assistant dean, the troubleshooter for the administration.

"She's on vacation," Carol said.

"Is Carla Beuhler in?"

At the last minute, Dean Beuhler had replaced Terri as a member of the interviewing committee. The other members had been Odette; Martha, an Italian instructor, who was a close friend of hers; and Raphael, the new language coordinator with an angel face and the attitude of a budding SS. He was also a close professional friend of Odette.

"She's in," Carol said. "You want to talk to her?"

The dean's cheery voice came over the phone. "Hello, Brigitte. What can I do for you?"

My voice quivered. I spoke slowly for control.

"Dean Beuhler, I would like to know why I haven't been found suitable for the full-time position in French. What transpired from the interview? After my teaching the maximum units allowed a part-timer...what...were the committee's remarks?"

At the other end of the line, Dean Beuhler was silent. I spoke again, unsure how to rephrase my question. "What official reason was given for passing me over?"

The dean cleared her throat briefly. The cheery tone now as gone as the smooth surface of a lake under a wind gust, her voice sharper, she answered, nevertheless, as if this were a routine question. "Brigitte, the applicants' files were sent to the president for her final approval."

"She would be the one to tell me?"

"No...She's gone till next month. The files must have been returned to the district. Let me check."

She put me on hold but soon returned. "Brigitte, the applicants' files have been returned. You should talk to the Director of Human Resources, Dr. Blinder. He's in charge of personnel. I'll give you his number."

There was another pause. When she returned, I asked, "Could you tell me the committee's findings yourself?"

"We've interviewed many people for several departments, as many as a hundred. And the files are back at the district. You have to talk to Dr. Blinder. He has the records."

It was now Saturday. I stood close to the ladder where my husband was standing to trim the Australian fern overgrowth clustering the arches, aiming the pruning shears with the precision of one who could tell at a glance the annual from the perennial. Dan looked at the arches. "What are you going to do about the college?" he asked, as if he had been assessing my options instead of his pruning.

I shrugged my shoulders, summarized once again for my benefit more than for his what we already knew. "I had been there longer than any other part-time instructor, always been told that I did a good job. I don't understand what happened."

Except perhaps: There had been Odette's memo of April 18, stating that any part-time instructor not attending two upcoming conferences on the natural approach to languages or not implementing this approach would not be re-hired.

Coming out of the classroom after my eight o'clock, I came upon George, a cordial full-time Spanish instructor. He was going toward his office, which he shared with Odette. She was not in yet. I stopped and asked him what he thought the memo meant.

"Don't you know what's going on?" He sounded angry. "If I were you, I'd go and ask Terri the meaning of that memo."

Taken aback by the brusqueness of his tone, I left to see the assistant dean. She invited me to sit down.

"This memo has nothing to do with you. It's a formality. Just attend the conference. Ask questions if you have any. Trust me. Your job isn't at stake."

"Trust me," she repeated when I left.

On the way to my car, I saw George waiting outside his office. I stopped to tell him what Terri had said.

"Did she mention a full-time position opening up in French to replace Odette while she is in Paris?" he asked.

"She didn't."

He shook his head. "I'm not supposed to know what's going on. But I understand enough French to have an idea. And I don't like what the two friends are plotting." He meant Odette and Raquelle.

He turned briskly and went into his office. I went to my car. As I backed out of my parking space, I saw, in my rear view mirror, that Raquelle's red Mazda was waiting to pull in.

I related the anecdote to Dan.

"Personally, I would want to talk to the president," he said.

"According to the dean, she's gone for the month."

"Of course," he said.

The president was a friend of Odette's. On French Day, the president sat at the same patio table as Odette and Raquelle. When Raphael, the coordinator, came in, he went directly to their table, hugging Odette and Raquelle as if they were the best of friends.

I sat at the next table with past and present students who had joined me, and later, with another newer part-time instructor. It was not until the president had left that Odette had looked in our direction and waved, then came over to talk.

I told Dan, "Carla Beuhler said that my questions should be directed to the personnel director at the District Office. He has the files."

"Someone to talk to at least," Dan said.

"I'll make an appointment with him. I like the idea of an impartial party taking a close look at my file records. I have a feeling that no one but Odette looked at them. That everyone else endorsed her decision. And I do need to know the reasons the panel members gave for passing me over."

Dan cocked his head, then moved to one of the arches. He entwined a fern around the base of the arch, setting it on its course. "Just be sure of your objective before you go see him."

"If it weren't for the students...and trying to save since, as a part-time instructor, I don't have a retirement..."

On Monday, I contacted Dr. Blinder's office. He was in. His secretary took my name and number, put me on hold, then put me through. He seemed to listen carefully to my explanations, asked me to repeat some. I had the feeling that he was taking notes. He promised to look into the records and to call me back.

When one week later, I had not heard from him, I called his office. The secretary answered. She said that he was in a conference, but that he would return my call in the afternoon.

He did not, so I called again on Tuesday. This time, he was taking an important phone call.

"I'd like to set up an appointment," I told the secretary.

Again, she asked my name and my number. She said that she would give it to him, and he would return my call later that day. Once more, the afternoon went by without his call.

I skipped over Wednesday to give him time to check my records if he had not already done so. I called on Thursday. He was in a conference. At ten on Friday, he was on the phone. At eleven, he wasn't in. "Did he leave a message for me?" I asked the secretary. "Set a conference date?"

"No," she said. "He hasn't."

"Would you ask him to call me this afternoon?"

"He's gone," she said. "Gone for the day."

"I'll call first...thing...Monday."

"Please do." Her tone was daring.

I was very much aware of an administrative procedure consisting of ignoring the problem in the hope that the objector would tire or be intimidated and go away. The more I was made to feel *persona non grata*, however, the more determined I became to seek an answer.

It was now Monday, the beginning of the third week since Blinder had said that he would call me back in a couple of days.

At nine o'clock, I called his secretary. She informed me that he would not be able to return my call today.

"Thank you very much," I said and hung up, and without a second thought, looked up the Teachers' Association's number in the telephone book. I called the representative, Mr. Oremor, to explain the situation.

"You certainly have a case," he said.

Then I told him of my difficulty in setting a conference with Dr. Blinder. Mr. Oremor laughed. "It's a typical scenario," he said. "What you have to do is write Dr. Blinder a letter stating that you question the hiring practices as implemented at the college, that you have tried in vain to set up a conference with him, and mail a copy to the president of the Teachers' Association, one to the president of the college, and one to me. That ought to get things moving. Give him ten days to reply. Let me know if you haven't heard from him by then."

That afternoon, I mailed the letter and the three copies.

On Wednesday, Dr. Blinder's secretary called. He would like to set up a conference with me. Would I be free to come Friday afternoon at two? "I'll be there," I said.

I gave a courtesy call to Mr. Oremor. "Good luck," he said.

At noon on Friday, before the meeting, I sat on the western edge of our patio. Minouche had followed me and settled muff-like under the shadeless Peruvian pepper tree. Her eyes scanned the yard, and then she turned her head toward me as if nodding her approval.

I looked at my watch. Twenty past twelve. I had a few more minutes before I had to go in and get ready for the interview. Ever so slightly, however, the shadow of the Peruvian pepper tree had stretched eastward, beyond the confines of the noon sun. I stood up. Minouche blinked. Good luck, she seemed to say. "Watch out for blackbirds," I answered.

At 1:45, I drove into the district office parking lot, parked on the side of the building. I checked my hair and make-up in the sun visor mirror and fluffed the fullness of my skirt. It was of a summer cotton, light brown with autumn leaves. I felt comfortable wearing it with my tan medium heel shoes. I wanted to be able to meet Dr. Blinder at exactly two o'clock per my appointment. I didn't want to forget the folder that I had brought along, where every point I intended to make was documented. I had a few minutes to wait. I placed it on my lap, leaned back against the seat of the car and closed my eyes to relax. When I opened them again, it was five to two. I grabbed my folder and at four till opened the door onto a wide, circular hall.

A receptionist behind a desk at the entrance barely raised her head. "May I help you?"

"My name is Brigitte Dulac. I have an appointment with Dr. Blinder at two."

She pointed to her right. "Halfway down the hall, the desk on your left will be his secretary's."

Wide and carpet-muffled, the hall seemed hallowed. I soon came upon another secretary who, from the elevation of her desk on a wide, circular pedestal to the right of an office, guarded its entrance with the watchfulness of a Cerberus.

I raised my head to speak to her. "I have an appointment at two with Dr. Blinder. My name is Brigitte Dulac."

"He's on the phone. Have a seat over there. He'll be with you right after the phone call."

I turned toward the cubicle where she had pointed, and in so doing, happened to glance into what might be Dr. Blinder's office. But his desk, probably burrowed against the farthest wall, was invisible from my standpoint. His voice, however, now came out as if in reply to a telephone interlocutor.

These things happen, I told myself. An inopportune incoming call before an appointment.

I entered a doorless, half-wall high, wood cubicle, reminiscent of a witness stand, and sat on a swivel chair near a wall-desk on which I set my file. I opened it to check the contents once more, but closed it right away because from across the entrance, the secretary towered above me like a judge over the accused.

Besides the April memo, the job description custom-fit for one person only, several unsolicited, spontaneous letters from grateful students, received throughout the years, saying how hard they had worked in the class, yet how much they had looked forward to each session were so present in my mind that reading them again now before seeing Dr. Blinder would have been distracting.

I let my chair swivel to face the wall of the main circular hallway. There were three paintings in pastel colors. The paintings were part of an orchestration pianissimo to soothe the waiter...me. As if ill, I were waiting in a doctor's office...and should forget my symptoms by the time he came in!

I glanced at his secretary. She was watching a computer screen, and occasionally typed on a silent keyboard. Then I looked at my watch. Ten minutes past two. The conversation should end soon, although the resounding voice coming out of the office and explaining at length the usage and distribution of a shipment of computer goods indicated that the conversation was not about to end.

As a countenance and to keep my mind alert—I should have brought a book—I opened my purse, took out my appointment book and scanned through the week. Nothing but this meeting was scheduled except for a trip to the grocery store, as the grocery list clipped to today's page reminded me.

Raising my eyes, I saw the secretary avert hers. I was in her field of vision. I sensed that when I was not looking, she watched me. For her benefit, I rewrote my grocery list, pausing after onions as if adding potatoes beneath required careful thought. When I looked at my watch, ten more minutes had passed.

Straightening up in my chair—ethical rules engraved in marble were not to be found here—I readjusted the strap of my purse on my shoulder and picked up my file off the desk.

Had the secretary pressed a button? Was there a hidden camera in this modern hall? The voice in the office came to an abrupt end. The secretary turned toward me.

"Dr. Blinder will see you," she said.

When I entered his office, he was crouched in a broad swivel armchair behind a wide executive desk, looking to his left toward the lower part of a bookshelf at something that I could not see from my standpoint. The bookshelf, at a 90 degree angle with the desk, stood much higher. Its high, wide back formed a dim recess with the adjacent and the opposite walls.

"Hello, Dr. Blinder," I said as I walked toward the desk.

He neither moved nor responded for a perceptible few seconds. I stopped and waited behind the armchair across the desk from him. He stood up. He was broad and tall, had blue eyes and blond hair turning white. He appeared to be in his fifties. Although I did not try to visualize him when I spoke to him on the phone, there was an air of unexpected affability about him.

"I'm Brigitte Dulac. I have an appointment with you."

He nodded. "Ron Blinder."

He extended a hand toward the waiting chair. I sat down, my knees and feet together. I placed my folder unopened before me on his desk. Except for a jigsaw-shaped pen and pencil holder, and a file—mine probably—already opened at his place, his desk was unencumbered.

"You're a hard man to see," I said. "If it were not for Mr. Oremor..."

"I'm very busy," he said. He sat down, pretending to leaf through my file. "How can I help you?"

I repeated what I had already stated to him in my letter. "I object to the hiring practices as they were implemented in the hiring of a full-time instructor at the college. After teaching at the college for thirteen consecutive years, I feel that I was very much qualified for that job—a one-semester job only—and I want to know what stopped me from getting it, what comments were made by the members of the interviewing committee."

"First," he said, "you have to realize that I receive the names of the candidates already selected by the committee and endorsed by the president of the college. Unless a problem is brought to my attention, I stamp the selection."

I made no reply.

He stood up, walked toward the bookshelf. "I already know about you," he said. He turned to look at me over his shoulder. I was looking up at him. His eyes met mine, then shifted away. I waited. He came back. "Good things."

"Oh?"

He walked toward the shelves again, explaining. "I've called the college and talked to Terri Will and to Dean Beuhler." He stopped talking. Came back. Paused. "They had only good things to say about you. They think very highly of you."

"Oh?" I could've argued the point, but instead I repeated, "I've been at the college thirteen years. That's why I want to know why I wasn't hired for the semester-long full-time position. What exactly were the comments that justified my not being hired when only last year, the full-time instructor asked me to take over her extra-curricular activities during a year-long absence? I wasn't to be paid for it, but she thought me competent enough. So much so that this year, she never bothered to observe my classes." I asked again, "What objections did the interviewing committee have against me? What official reason did they give?"

He came back toward his chair, sat down. He sifted through my file, held a page in his hands, glanced through it, put it back down. He straightened up, looked at me. "Sometimes it's a very fine line. I've looked at your file carefully, and I've looked at Raquelle's file. Your records are identical. You could have been sisters."

My hands flew up. "Oh no; we couldn't. Not even with the age difference." I stopped, aware that I had lost my poise. I put my hands back on my lap, but my heart was pounding. He waited for me to continue.

"I'm sorry. I didn't mean to interrupt you." I was sitting straighter, and I felt that my stare had hardened as Minouche's stare does when she senses the threat of blackbirds invading our yard.

He now sifted through a folder that I had not noticed before. He said, after scanning one of the pages, "She taught at the elementary level…and…" he looked at my folder. "You taught in grade school."

"In France. Second grade in a public elementary school."

"She taught in a private school. As a teacher's aide."

I made no comment.

He continued on, mentioning bachelor's degrees, master's degrees. He did not mention honors or honor societies or letters of recommendation. "You could be sisters," he said again, but this time I did not react. I was still awaiting an answer to my first question about the committee's findings.

He placed his forearms on my folder, leaned across the desk toward me. "You reacted strongly when I first made this statement. Why?"

116

I felt as if he were stalking my answer; as if he expected me to bring forth my double major, English in addition to French, and the honors in both so that he may say that they too were identical. But I also knew that English was no more relevant to teaching French than honors were to teaching well.

Our eyes met.

"We do not have the same experience. The same number of years of experience at the college level. At the same college. Thirteen versus one."

He swiveled from right to left along a half-moon trajectory until the right arm of his chair rested parallel with his desk, and he faced the bookshelf. He traveled the semi-circle back to face me. "The number of years is not the main consideration. Sometimes, it has to do with methodology."

I had two points to make. "As you know, I have been teaching here for a long time." I moved toward the edge of my chair. "If my teaching wasn't good enough, then the college is derelict for employing me that long, for offering me to teach the advanced classes next semester. As a taxpayer, I object."

He ignored my remark. His eyebrows and one corner of his lips rose. It was my uncle's smile when, as director for a bank, he dismissed a pointless remark.

His chair traveled again along the 180 degree curve. Returned. When he faced me, I resumed. "If a job description was conceived…was contrived to fit an applicant as tightly as a surfer's wetsuit fits the surfer, I believe it is favoritism. And the carefully construed description of the methodology *was* the surfer's wetsuit. I object to the use of a public institution as if it were a family owned business."

I told him about the April memo. "I use the method they proclaim, the communicative approach—no English, no grammatical explanations—when they work best for my students. But I resort to some English and some explanations when they are necessary."

His hands against the edge of the desk, he pushed his chair away, then scooted forward, a glitter in his eyes. He placed his elbows on the desk. His hands joined to form a cathedral. It slowly pivoted and pointed toward me.

"When I was in college and took Spanish, we never spoke a word of Spanish! Now people travel. They want to use the language."

I nodded in agreement. He stopped for me to talk. "We can't analyze a language as a coroner does a corpse. I agree." He smiled. I continued. "I have attended several conferences and workshops on the method at many institutions. The proponents of the method can't agree whether to use English at all in the classroom. Whether to explain grammar or incorporate it without explanations. A language without grammar—at least some grammar—is like a tree without a trunk. The leaves lie in decaying heaps."

As if it were self-propelled, the chair traveled this way and that. "I hear you," he conceded after it had stopped.

"The objective is to bring students to the point where they can communicate. I do that. Using some English when need be. I bring them to the standard level...and above. We work hard, but most of the time we have fun doing it."

I leaned back against my chair, moved my folder from his desk to my lap. I did not feel now like bringing out the testimonial of past students, of other supervisors. Besides, some of the letters were enclosed with my job application. He would only say that Raquelle had identical recommendations.

I moved forward again. "Even if Raquelle had in some way an objective edge over me during her interview, I was there longer. I have more experience with our students. When there was no job, no compensation, I was offered the responsibilities and accepted some. Now that there is a full-time job *with pay*, a one-semester job only, someone who has taught there one semester as opposed to my thirteen years gets it."

He leaned forward. "Sometimes, then...during an interview...it's a matter of dress. I could write books about people who do not dress properly for an interview..."

His remark seemed off the mark, but I listened. Then it occured to me. He meant it for me. Perhaps I did not dress properly. I wore a summer linen suit. Then...was I not dressed as I should be today? I was getting nowhere. I picked up the folder on my lap.

He extended a hand, intimating to wait. He stood up.

"I see that you are a very competent, dedicated professional," he said, emphasizing and pausing between each word. I
was surprised. I put the folder back on my lap. He sat down,
took a piece of paper out of a drawer, set it before him. "What do
you want me to do?" he asked, a pen in hand.

"I would like three things." He nodded. "But first, I
want to make it clear that I do not want the job. Even if it could
be offered to me now, I would not accept it."

He raised his head. His face, however, remained expres-
sionless. He was still poised to write my requests.

"I want to see that the college adopt objective hiring practices, and that they be enforced so as to deter manipulations behind the scenes." I was pleased that my voice had not faltered.

"You've got it." He wrote.

"Hopefully, it will help others."

He stopped writing. "Why not you? There will be other
occasions, other studies in Paris."

"I would like you to grant me a transfer to another college within this district. This is my second request."

"I can do that." He put his pen down on the desk, and his
chair swiveled. But it stopped midway on its ellipse and returned.
"Actually, I can't. Part-time faculty cannot be transferred. You
have to go through the process of reapplying. What I can do is
give you a letter of recommendation. Of course, they may not
need anyone."

"Then I must resign from my part-time job here. My
husband and I are far from wealthy. As you know, I have no
retirement and no social security...and I like the students. But I
cannot return. My third request has to do..."

His face was red, and his chair started on another trip.
"Now why would you do that?" he asked, scolding the shelves at
the end of the journey. "Why?" he repeated when he was, again,
facing me. "Do you know how long it would take the college to
replace you?"

I raised my hand and snapped my fingers. "Like that."

"Exactly. Then why? One thing I have learned from
looking at applicants' files is that teachers of foreign languages
have the best resumes. It's a fact. The competition is fierce."

119

He leafed through other applications. "I recently applied for the job of County Superintendent," he said. "I was one of three finalists. I came close, but I didn't get it. I am not quitting my job for that. I feel badly, but it was a good experience. I learned from it. I hope to reapply some day."

"It's not the same," I said. "Yours is a permanent, full-time job. With benefits, I presume. Mine is part-time without any. The college offered a one-semester position. It would have entitled me to a meager retirement. In addition, they wanted someone familiar with college teaching. I was familiar with that college and had good enrollment at the beginning as well as at the end of the semester despite a reputation for being a demanding teacher. The students liked my classes, and I liked teaching them."

I could've added that I don't have enough time left to reapply, invoked ageism in addition to favoritism—but he was still leafing through the files.

"Actually, one of the five applicants...there were only five...had a doctorate degree in French. And college experience. He did not even get an interview. I wonder why. I would have at least interviewed him. Wouldn't you?"

"That's my point," I said.

"I hear you." He wrote a note to himself. "I still don't understand why you wouldn't go back. You like the students. You are highly esteemed at the college."

"The administration has no right to claim that."

His face reddened, and once more, he undertook the pilgrimage to the shelves. I lacked the proper distance to evaluate why my words, at this time, had caused him this discomfort. He was back now. He put his forearms on the desk and leaned toward me. But he did not speak.

"I'm judging on actions *not* taken," I was explaining, when his secretary walked in. Looking at her watch, she placed a note in front of him. He pushed it aside.

"Your being there is a reminder of how wrong they were."

The secretary left.

"A reminder not to do that again..."

Going back was tempting. The students—I could hear Brian leaning from the second floor balustrade of the art building where my class was held: "I hear those steps. I could recog-

nize those steps anywhere." *And Allyson's voice, from behind him, echoing: "Moi aussi, je...how do you say 'recognize' in French, Mrs. Dulac?" And another time, Brian: "Here are those steps again."*

"...Not to repeat the mistake. Sometimes...our feelings, our pride..."

"It's not a matter of pride."

"Well, then? Think. The semester will go by, and the full-time instructor will be back. Things will be as they were before."

I looked at him, but he was not being facetious. "To make a statement," I said.

"You got me there." There was no smirk on his face. He stood up, looked outside the window, then sat down again. His chair swiveled to and fro. "I would like you to reconsider. I want you to promise me that you will at least reconsider."

I had not anticipated his request, let alone his insisting. If he feared my attempting a lawsuit against the college for unfair practices, I am not the suing type. I was reluctant, and my shoulders rose. "My...third request...is...for the committee's findings. I do want to know their objections against me."

He added this last request to the list. "I'll telephone the president when she returns, and I'll get back to you."

"Thank you." I stood up.

He stood up too. "But promise me that you will reconsider." He came around his desk and extended his hand to me. "Promise me to give it thought," he insisted as he shook my hand.

"I will," I conceded, annoyed at myself for delaying the decision, and yet glad that it was not final.

On the way to the door, he stepped inside the dim recess formed by the back of the bookshelves and the two walls. "Would you like a bubble gum?" he asked in the tone of someone proposing a toast, as he bent over a bubble-gum dispenser on a table back of the shelves.

I smiled. Or believe I did. "No, thanks."

He saw me to the door. "Don't forget to reconsider."

His voice followed me around and past the secretary at her elevated desk. She glanced at her watch and at me. I looked at mine. It was past four-thirty. No one now sat at the desk facing the entrance. I hastened toward my car on the side of the building. At the corner I stopped, startled, because in the space next to mine in the otherwise deserted parking lot was Raquelle's red Mazda. Bits of the conversation with Binder and the puzzle of Raquelle's presence at this time at the district office bounced through my head when I arrived home.

Had she been summoned? Where had she been kept hidden while I left what seemed to be an almost empty building? What did Blinder intend for her and me to do if I had not indicated my intent to resign? Work out differences, as if that had been the matter? Or had she come to sign her contract, her web of friends extending as far as the district office?

Dan was not home yet, but Minouche greeted me at the door. I got rid of my purse and my folder and let her climb on my shoulder. Carrying her rifle-like as Dan called it, I stepped outside on the patio. The arches opened today on a yellowish-blue smog. I should ask Dan to let the leaves grow inside again. The evening sea breeze, however, was rising and the fern nodded hello.

I sat on the patio's edge and Minouche jumped off from my shoulder onto the grass. She stretched and settled by my feet. Soon after, I heard Dan's car stop in the driveway. The screen door behind me slid open.

"How did it go?" Dan asked, sitting down next to me.

Minouche crawled between us.

I told him about my waiting to see Blinder, my long conversation with him, the option still available to me, the puzzle of Raquelle's car next to mine. "He will ask the president when she returns what the committee's annotations were."

"That's nonsense," Dan said. "There were none. Wasn't your file before him? You're not going back, are you?" Dan asked.

Dan and I looked at each other and smiled.

"Not me," I said.

"That's fine." He put his arm around my shoulders.

Taking off like an arrow, Minouche chased blackbirds alighting on the fence.

Professional

by Andrew Guy

As an adjunct writing instructor at a New York City community college, I saw myself as the last academic opportunity for ambitious, inner-city kids whose high schools had let them down. When a cynical African-American student remarked in anger and frustration that the institution didn't give a damn, and that the system was racist, I told the students that I, a middle class white guy, was part of the system, and that I very much cared.

Teaching in the inner city had its frustrations. If the budget got cut or tuition increases sent enrollments tumbling, the system laid me off. Each time I was rehired, the phone call typically came two days before the first class. As a part-timer, I was rarely on campus for paydays; in order to have my checks mailed home, I had to give the school stamped, self-addressed envelopes.

Earning $2000 a semester per course meant having to hold down two other part-time jobs. It didn't help that part-timers, who outnumbered full-timers in this college three to one, had to sign what we called "The Contract on Adjuncts," making us promise to accept no more than two course assignments per semester across the entire 21-campus University system because a bigger course load would have made us full-timers by law—entitled to job security, health benefits and a living wage.

Faced with steady cost-of-living increases and a pay rate that stayed flat in all my three jobs, I had no choice but to log more time as a temp and a tutor, and to turn less attention to my own writing. My first responsibility, like a parent's, remained to "my kids."

Nevertheless, time pressures motivated me to make certain changes in my teaching. I decided to reorder the same textbook each semester rather than take the time to try out new ones— and, unexpectedly, I became so conversant in its lessons and essays that my skill in leading discussions actually improved. Instead of losing hundreds of hours inventing exercises for my students and reading every draft of their papers, I started simply supervising as *they* designed activities and responded to each other's writing. With this approach, I happened to conform to the latest pedagogy about student empowerment; give composition students freedom and responsibility, and they'll learn to like writing, write more, and subsequently write better. In short, I had successfully wedded apathy--overworked and exhausted as I was--with professional pride.

In my eight a.m. class, Shirley had perfect attendance but never volunteered a word. Whenever I called on her, she lifted her head from her desk near the door, glanced at the clock and gazed at me with contempt. But she did begrudgingly participate. Reading aloud, she spoke with a poise which convinced me she had ability. Her written work was better than average.

Toward the end of the semester, Shirley submitted a short personal essay on coping with postpartum depression. Engaging and exceptionally well informed, the essay described old biases ("Many problems once dismissed as 'women's troubles' are, today, recognized as legitimate medical issues...") and offered tacit advice ("If diagnosed properly, postpartum depression can be treated and cured"). It was impressive stuff coming from a woman who didn't have children. Shirley had not attached any drafts either—though as a policy I never marked down for the lack, since a few good students invariably lost or forgot them, and I no longer read them anyway. The diction in Shirley's paper was eloquent and sure, and the grammar flawless, exhibiting none of her chronic troubles with comma splices, subject-verb agreement, faulty parallelism and the 'ed' suffix. All in all, it represented quite an achievement; the paper read just like a pamphlet from a clinic waiting room.

Plagiarism is generally regarded as the most dastardly academic crime. It warrants failure—certainly of the paper and probably of the course. It could mean expulsion from the college. With stakes like that, the crime must be proven, the plagiarized source found—a task which could take many hours. Instead, I wrote a note on Shirley's paper to see me after class.

"Yeah, what?" She heaved her hips to the side and glared at me.

I held up the paper. "Is this your writing?"

"Yeah. Why?"

"It doesn't sound like your writing." I let the silence lengthen. She just stood there and smirked. "Did anyone help you with it? The Writing Center?"

"No." She stared dispassionately at me.

"Look," I said, deciding to give her—and myself—a means off the hook. "I'm willing to believe you misunderstood the directions. But you'll have to redo this. The assignment was meant to be all your own writing."

"It's all mine."

Amazed, I smiled. We both knew she had plagiarized. Yet Shirley had me, since what could I do without proof? As I stood there, I wondered why I tolerated students like Shirley— enrolled to gather credits, not to learn. I wondered why I tolerated a perpetually broken photocopy machine and a salary lower than what Shirley earned bagging groceries. She had me all right. She knew perfectly well I wouldn't bother tracking down that pamphlet.

And suddenly I realized that Shirley regarded me as the enemy. She didn't give a damn about the class, and she also knew—as I had not realized until that very moment—that *I* didn't give a damn either, not even about so much as trying to teach her the basics of right and wrong. Was I the reason she didn't care? I felt my smile warp into what Shirley must have recognized as a sneer.

"Yeah, what?" she prodded.

"Well, Shirley, it's unbelievable how you've improved," I said, laying into her when I should have been scorning the under-funded sham of a public education system that had corrupted us both. "What fine writing! Infinitely better than anything you've ever done. This here?" —I rapped the paper with the back my hand much too sharply—"Professional."

Recognizing the end of my career as an effective adjunct, I bent over the paper with my felt-tip pen and slashed the three lines of a big, red letter "A". I said, "You must feel very proud."

Stealth Justice

by J. L. Schneider

The plagiarism was clear, irrefutable, unambiguous as black and white. Assigned a Compare and Contrast paper in my English composition class, the student copied an essay from the remedial textbook he'd used the previous semester, substituted the name of a town and a few streets, then handed it in as his own. After doing my own compare and contrast of the two essays, I gave the student a zero for his paper, which, under the Code of Conduct outlined by my college, was the least of the punishments he could have received, the worst being expulsion from my class. Both the Dean of Academic Affairs and the head of my English Department corroborated my assessment of the plagiarized paper, the former saying it was the worst case of plagiarism he'd ever seen, the latter saying that the student should have been given a zero for stupidity—copying a text that every English teacher was familiar with—instead of stealing. It was an open and shut case. Except for one detail. The student was African-American, and I was a white adjunct.

The proof of the student's transgression was incontrovertible. By all objective standards, the racial discrimination suit the student filed against me and the college should never have been brought in the first place, such was the overwhelming evidence against him. So how did it happen, and why was it that I was put through an ordeal that made me seriously question my ability, then my desire, to do my job, which I've always taken great pride in?

The answer, I believe, is simple. The context from which that answer arose through many specious guises, is not.

It is a context, especially noticeable in my students, of an increasingly faultless society. It is the context of a balmy, even heady, ethos of blame and abnegation that seems to hover in no one place, yet can appear as solid as a subpoena at the next slip of the tongue. It is the context of fear—a fear of others, which is ultimately a fear of oneself—which enables a student to rise, without a shred of supporting evidence, through the grievance procedures of an English Department, a college, and proceed to the federal level. It is a context—even as that context has helped deserving people gain justice—that has given rise to a malady far worse than the cancer the context was supposed to cure. The cancer I speak of, of course, is racism; the even worse disease, in my opinion, is inculpability.

Scientists tell us we have a genetic predisposition to bigotry, racism, a fear of the "other." In our pre-history, anyone from outside one's group was considered a threat to that group. Strangers were seen as competitors and depletors of the limited gene pool of one's community, serious business when survival is at stake. Consequently, there arose a psychological fear of the other, and in those days threats, and sometimes bloodletting, were enough to keep the interlopers at bay (even as nature was pulling the genetic rug out from under our clay feet, introducing diversity, which would insure the perpetuation of those very fears we now use against each other.)

Today, we use lawyers instead of clubs, but the basic ingredient in the fear of others is still blame. The Nazis knew it. The Rwandans knew it. The Serbs and Croats knew it. It is one thing to say "I hate that person." It is when one says "I blame that person" that the first steps toward action (revenge, lynching, genocide) are taken. I'm sure my student hated me—I saw it in his eyes. It's not an unusual emotion to see in a profession where one is constantly grading others. It was when my student started blaming me, however, that the disease took hold of his heart and mind.

It's unpopular these days for a white man to talk openly and critically about race-relations in this country, as if, first, he is assumed to be a part of the problem, and second, if he's not a part of the problem, he has no right to talk about something he can't possibly understand. It is often assumed, especially if he's in a position of power (like a teacher), that privilege granted his position, and that that privilege was acquired by treading on the backs of everyone who was less privileged than he, i.e. non-white. I've heard the argument that a white man in power is automatically keeping people of color (if not consciously then subconsciously, his mind tapping into this nation's historical precedence for racism) from rising above their station. That is, of course, if the issue is race. Which, in the case of my cheating student, it wasn't. But which it was quickly turned into, the motivation also seeming to arise subconsciously.

I run a strict class, and I raise the bar high for my students. All of them. By the time they enter college, I don't believe that students are children to be coddled. I believe, as Lincoln is supposed to have said, that eventually everyone is responsible for his own face, that one does not blame the world for the lines of joy or sorrow we show to others. My students are adults, capable (one would think) of understanding rules, goals, and consequences. I explain those rules clearly at the beginning of each class, expect them to be followed, and explain the consequences if they're not. Discipline, I tell them, if it was extrinsic before, must now be called upon from within. In essence, I ask them to be responsible for their actions, at least in the very small world of an English composition class.

The day I asked my student to stay after class to discuss his plagiarized paper, I had both his essay and the text he plagiarized on my desk. I had a copy of the Code of Conduct. I even had a dictionary, in case he didn't know what the word *plagia-*

rism meant. I felt no malice toward him; if anything, I was sympathetic. Cheating, any crime, is usually an act of desperation, and I was not immune to those students of mine who were struggling, who were desperate to do well, even if they didn't understand the basic principle of hard work equaling reward. Unfortunately, my student hadn't grasped that concept. He was often absent from class, had numerous excuses, and hadn't been incorporating the simplest of techniques to better his writing, consequently, his grade. Nevertheless, I was willing to listen, even as I considered, as a practicing writer, the act of plagiarism to be one of the most egregious sins in the field of writing.

After being confronted with the evidence of his transgression, and after I explained exactly what plagiarism was, my student's first reaction was to try and grab his paper out of my hand. He said he wanted to show it to a friend. Surprised by the sudden tug of war, I said that that wasn't possible, and held onto his paper for several long, tense moments. He finally released his grip, then started to angrily collect his books. I tried to force the issue, quickly, because he was about to go, and I hadn't anticipated this turn of events. Considering the glaring proof of his guilt, I had expected our meeting to be nothing less than immediate contrition on his part. But he was having none of it—he refused to look at his paper and the original essay, at the verbatim sentences in the two, or to even discuss the ramifications of academic dishonesty. The only thing he said as he left the classroom, which also took me aback, because it was muttered with great malice and venom, was, "So a black person can't have those experiences, huh?" referring to the ones he had plagiarized. Then he was gone.

About a month later, my department head informed me that the student had started in motion the complaint proceedings for his discrimination suit (this after I twice tried to talk to the student, without success, to discuss the matter further), proceedings which eventually reached the civil rights division of the United States Department of Education. The investigation took over six months, during which time I had innumerable meetings with my college's representative handling the case, and one very long, strenuous interrogation by an investigator from the DOE.

It's not necessary to talk here about the personal toll these events exacted on me, how gun-shy I was the following semester (as the investigation continued) when I first stepped into a classroom, or how angry I was at being turned into a criminal while the person who committed the crime was being viewed as a victim. Nor is it important to talk about the hollow victory I felt when I was handed the DOE's nine page exoneration. What's important, it seems, is still the context.

I did, indeed, come to see that student as a victim, but not the kind he thought he was, or the kind that our society now rallies behind on a regular basis. Instead, I came to see an evil that I thought existed only on talk shows and in the memoirs of our dysfunctional literati. I came to see that that young man had, somewhere along the course of his life, been sold a bill of goods. He was told, probably not overtly, but through the relatively recent institutionalization of inculpability and the illusion of justice awarded to the inculpable—the disease replacing the cancer—that he had every right to blame someone else for his shortcomings. He was lead to believe that being oppressed made him virtuous. And that mantle of virtue, like the non-existent mantle of privilege attributed to his oppressor, is an illusion.

That student was not an exception in my classes, nor was he unique because he was black. He was merely the loudest. I have seen the same need to blame authority, the teacher, the other, in every one of my classes, regardless of race. It fills me with despair, almost dread. I have begun to fear for a generation of young people and the socio-litigious context that enables, even encourages, their supposedly inalienable right to censure. I fear for all of us if we begin to believe that the blindfold across the eyes of Justice means not "I am blind," rather, "I am blameless."

I continue to teach, and continue to exhort the virtue, the *necessity*, of individual responsibility. And because of this intransigence, I fully expect, as an adjunct professor whose position is always tenuous in higher education, especially in a context of institutional abnegation, that someday I will be fired. I don't feel the least bit sorry for myself. Once again, I despair for the context. A context already firmly in place, from the frightened underlings who must mollify every assertion of discrimination lest they be thought insensitive, or worse, sued, all the way to the federal courts. A context that enables any one of us motivated by fear of self-reflection and responsibility to make enough noise, properly pitched to the victim's song, until that squeaky wheel gets so well oiled by the need to placate it runs over the rest of us without so much as a whisper.

This is stealth justice. It happens quietly. Subtly. Furtively. The overt consequence of such justice is the illusory ardor of wrongs being righted. But stealth justice—the need to blame others while gaining recompense from everyone but the guilty—is a ravenous beast. It is consumptive. And it eventually starts eyeing its closest allies.

A Night in the Adjunct Life

by Tim Waggoner

One of the best pieces of advice about teaching I ever received was "be flexible." That bit of wisdom has served me in good stead numerous times during my career as an adjunct English instructor, but never more so than one summer night several years ago when, while teaching a beginning composition course, I had to flex like I'd never flexed before!

It was a hot muggy July evening, the first meeting for a weekly composition course I was teaching for a local community college (one of three different schools I was working for at the time). The class was located at one of the college's off campus sites, a high school on the far north side of town. I was driving a '79 Toyota Corolla, sans air conditioning, and by the time I pulled into the school's parking lot, my shirt was soaked with sweat, and my hair plastered to my head. I parked, went inside and checked my appearance in a restroom mirror. I looked as if I'd decided to swim a couple laps in my work clothes before coming to class.

Not exactly the best impression to make on the first night. I washed my face and neck at the sink and then tried to do something about my sweat-matted blond hair. I finally gave up when I realized there wasn't much I could do beyond combing my hair and waiting for it to dry.

I retrieved the class roster from the site clerk (who was kind enough not to comment on my bedraggled appearance) and headed off for class. The building was virtually deserted, and I had to make my way through an empty maze of hallways lined with day glow orange carpeting. I located my room and entered, trying to carry myself as much like a professional teacher as I could, despite looking like a drowned rodent wearing a necktie.

Things started off well enough. I went over the roster and syllabus, then launched into an introduction to the writing process. But before I could finish, the room's speaker crackled to life, and a booming voice blasted forth.

"WE'RE JUST ABOUT READY TO BEGIN, FOLKS, SO YOU ALL SHOULD TAKE YOUR SEATS AND GET SET TO PLAY SOME BINGO!"

A couple of the students laughed knowingly while the rest looked at me quizzically.

"They have Bingo in the cafeteria during the summer," one of my clued-in students explained.

"EVERYBODY GET YOUR CARDS SET UP!" urged the echoing voice of the announcer. It sounded as if God Himself were preparing to call out the numbers.

"It'll go on for a couple of hours," another student put in.

I sighed. "I'll be right back."

I left the room and headed for the site clerk's office. Meanwhile, the announcer's voice echoed up and down the halls— "O-6...N-17..."—making the very air vibrate. I realized that every speaker in the entire building was blaring out the Bingo game at top volume.

The site clerk told me they were working on the problem, and as if to illustrate her point, two men ran frantically by and into a room where I presumed the controls for the intercom system were kept. After several moments, they ran back out, even more frantic now, and disappeared down another hallway. The Bingo game continued uninterrupted.

"I-4...B-3..."

The site clerk assured me that the two running men—whose identities I never did learn—would solve the problem in short order, and that I should return to my class and cope as best I could in the meantime.

Back in the classroom, the students were sitting patiently. They couldn't talk because the Bingo game was too loud. *Be flexible*, I told myself. I gave them a reading assignment, having to write it on the board because they couldn't hear my instructions over the blasting intercom. Of course, only half the students had purchased their textbooks before class, so everyone had to buddy up.

Twenty minutes passed, and still the Bingo blared on, the sound vibrations rattling the windows and thrumming through the floor and up into our feet. My ears were starting to ache by this point, and a number of students had finished their reading—or abandoned it due to an inability to concentrate through the din—and were using notebook paper to play along with the game.

"G-13."

One of my students jumped up and shouted, "Bingo!" and the rest of the class applauded.

Enough was enough. "Everyone pick up your books!" I shouted over the announcer. "We're moving outside!"

I led the students through the hall maze, past the site clerk's office, and out the front entrance. The glass doors closed shut behind us and, while the Bingo game could still be heard, it was blessedly muffled.

I smiled in relief. "Okay, everyone sit down, and we'll pick up where we left off." The students settled onto the concrete, and we started talking about the importance of purpose and audience in writing.

Less than five minutes later, it started to rain. And due to the building's design, there was little overhang to provide shelter, certainly not enough for the entire class.

I looked at my watch. Only twenty minutes left. *To hell with it*, I thought.

"Class dismissed," I said, trying not to sound as exasperated as I felt. Shaking their heads and laughing at our bad luck, the students gathered their texts and notebooks and headed for their cars. I stood under the overhang and watched as the first of the students began driving away. Suddenly, the rain slackened and stopped. It had been a passing summer cloudburst, nothing more.

Then the glass door opened, and the site clerk stuck her head out. "They've got the intercom fixed. You can bring your class back inside now." She didn't seem to notice that I had no class left to bring in.

I thanked her as politely as I could manage, and she left. As I watched the last of my students drive off, I realized something. I had forgotten to give them next week's assignment.

I picked up my briefcase and trudged toward my sauna of a car. It looked like I was going to get the chance to be flexible again next week.

"Sit Down When Shots Are Fired!"

by Kathryn Albrecht

A fter the gates slam shut, I cross the grass as the moonlight glistens off the barbed wire and two signs greet me: "SIT DOWN WHEN SHOTS ARE FIRED!" and "INMATES APPROACHING AIRCRAFT WILL BE SHOT!"

I am an adjunct college instructor at a maximum security prison. I teach writing and literature. Because of my career choice, I consciously bring the potential for violence into my life on a regular basis. Working in this environment requires an interesting balance between ignoring this violence and being aware of it. In order to enter the prison, I must in some sense ignore the potential for violence. I must ignore the memorial to the guards and other employees who have been killed. I must ignore the assortment of confiscated homemade weapons displayed in the gatehouse. When people discover that I teach in a prison, their question is always, "Aren't you afraid?" My answer is, "No." Most of my time spent behind the walls is not spent in fear. I couldn't do my job if it was. Then again to be safe, I must be aware of my surroundings at all times. I haven't had to hit the ground when shots were fired yet, but instructors who have been teaching longer than me have had to.

As a teacher in this setting, I strive to give my students an experience that is as close to a classroom on the outside as I possibly can. However, it doesn't seem useful or right to ignore their living conditions. Students come to class with black eyes. They disappear from class because they are put in segregation. They disappear because "something is going on in the cell house." Or they just disappear. When they leave my classroom, they return to a seven by eleven foot cell. They return to shakedowns, lockdowns, gang violence and a general lack of control. In the classroom, I ask them to be responsible—to be responsible for doing their work, for their own learning experience. Yet in the rest of their lives, they are expected to take no responsibility. They are told what to do and when to do it. They cannot open a door without permission. The process of institutionalization is an insidious one. I've heard my students joke about standing in front of a door waiting for a guard to open it only to discover it was open the whole time.

While we are in the classroom, we can pretend for a while that we are in a "normal" college classroom. That is, if we can ignore the guard in the hall who believes, "that animals should just be locked in their cages," or the one on the way out who says, "Ya learn 'em anything tonight?" If we can ignore the GED teacher across the hall who believes, "It's too late for most of these guys," who dreams of winning the lottery, who doesn't even pretend to teach anymore—just turns on the television or computer games.

When the prison goes on lockdown, prisoners remain in their cells twenty-four hours a day, and I must walk the cell houses to collect or pass out assignments. The length of the lockdown depends upon the cause. If an officer has been beaten or stabbed, the lockdown will be a long one. If a prisoner has been hurt, the lockdown may only last a day or two.

The cell houses are noisy—televisions (sometimes two to a cell), radios, tape decks and voices vie for attention. The smell is a combination of beans cooking and insecticide. Two men are housed in a seven by eleven foot cell, unless a prisoner has enough status to warrant a single. Strings wind their way down the hall like the tail of a kite. This is the way prisoners pass notes to one another—tied to the string and handed down the gallery from cell to cell. It is from this practice that correspondence between inmates got the nickname "kites." One of my students is on the phone with his "auntie" when I arrive. He sits on the bed in his cell—the phone is plugged in down the hall. The luxury of both a phone and a single cell indicates that this is a man with some power. A couple of days later, I receive a message from him on my answering machine, which I ignore.

It is more difficult to walk after dinner. I slip and slide on the milk and food that has been strewn about the walkway. I hold the cell bars in my hands, sometimes standing on the bottom bar, to try to get an unobstructed view of my student's face. Some students—most students—are happy to see me. A few peer out hesitantly from behind the blanket covering their door, embarrassed to encounter me under these conditions. The decorations in the cells range from centerfolds and cars to family photos and religious icons. Most prisoners have blankets hung over their doors and around their toilets for privacy.

Mirrors come out of the cells as I walk down the gallery. Everyone wants to talk to me—especially because I am a woman— and I have to be careful to focus on my students, or I will never make it off one gallery. I make the mistake of talking to a stranger. His hand grazes my breast as I lean on his cell. I reposition myself out of his reach and continue to tell him what classes are being offered next semester. I sense movement and feel very uncomfortable. I think he is masturbating, but I don't look for confirmation. I move quickly to the next cell.

I don't expect to accomplish much the first day back to class after a long lockdown. It is difficult for the students to focus. The violence of their past and present lives is reflected in other subtle and not so subtle ways. In a response to *Death of a Salesman*, one student discusses his own father's suicide. He offers a revised ending for the play, one in which Willy Loman kills his oppressors and family, like "the people at the post offices." The student writes that he did not discuss Willy's wife in his essay because "All women are bitches." Another student comments that he doesn't ever want to be forced to read plays like the

139

ones we read in class ever again, plays that deal with homosexuality, interracial marriage and the black power struggle. He concludes his response by saying that, "It is strange with so many good white playwrights, that we read about the black race." His sentiment is echoed by a student who responds to *Raisin* by saying that he was proud to be a member of the "tribe of Caucasus," and that there was nothing he could learn from other cultures.

One of the classes in the composition series allows me to teach a unit on animal rights. The prisoners at the maximum-security prison are less empathetic to the subject than my students at the medium security prison. They are offended by the comparison that some scholars make between the oppression of animals and the oppression of Blacks and find it difficult to be concerned about the treatment of animals given their own life circumstances. The subject of animal rights brings out stories of atrocities they have committed against animals; cats set on fire, dogs fed Alka Seltzer and left to die, yet few students are able to make any connections between this violence and other violence they have committed or that is committed against them.

The issue of ignoring or focusing on violence is raised again concerning my students' crimes. Do I want to know what their case is? Does it matter? Does it affect my ability to be a good instructor? In general population, the unspoken rule seems to be, "Don't ask. Don't tell."

When I am not teaching gen pop, I teach in the protective custody (PC) unit. PC is comprised of inmates whose lives would be in danger in gen pop. They may be in danger for a number of reasons—gambling debts, lack of gang affiliation, small physical stature, or white supremacist beliefs. Not a good idea to be in gen pop if you have a white pride tattoo. Any transsexuals or transvestites would, of course, be housed in PC.

While teaching in protective custody, I discovered that these inmates were more forthcoming about their crimes. In a class of about ten students, I realized that at least five of them had committed multiple murders. This class turned out to be one of the best classes I have taught at the prison. These students were some of the brightest, funniest and most articulate students I had met. One of my more surreal experiences was watching two of my students—both in for murder—who had come to class slightly inebriated, sit in the back row and sing the Barney theme song. You know, the big purple dinosaur on TV. "I love you/You love me/We're a happy family."

A Lover's Complaint

by Gary P. Henrickson

I'm leaving you again, Academia. I've tried to make this relationship work, but nothing that I've done seems to please you. I can't go on this way forever, taking your odd free moments--a section here, a section there. I want to be married to you. I want a full-time, tenure track position. If it doesn't work out after five or six years, fine, deny me tenure, we'll get a divorce, and I'll leave you alone. But you're not willing to work on this relationship, and I can't live with it. Goodbye.

Why won't you love me?

You said my experience in foreign schools doesn't count; you said it's not the same as teaching in the states.

It's true that teaching overseas is different. I once taught a graduate seminar on the veranda of a building because no classroom was available. I taught in classrooms where there was no light, no heat, no chalkboard, no modem. I taught in a classroom where there was a soldier posted at every window and a tank at the front gate. It's true. Teaching overseas is different.

You said that my experience didn't qualify as multi-cultural.

I taught in Yemen for two and one-half years, in Syria for one year, in Taiwan for three years, in Russia for one-half year, in Poland for one summer. I have lived, taught, slept, eaten and drunk as a foreigner. I have studied French, Arabic, Chinese, and Russian. I can direct a taxi in three different dialects of Arabic; I can find bread in a Russian city, no mean feat. I can haggle prices in Chinese. And you tell me I'm not multi-cultural.

You tell me I haven't published enough.

I have published as much or more as some of the faculty who sit on your hiring committees. More than that, I have published while having little or no access to modern libraries. In Yemen, libraries are quiet places to pray and chew quat. In Russia, books are almost non-existent and no periodical indexes of any kind exist. In Taiwan, the best library is in Taipei, a day's journey, but even this library would not qualify as a college library by your standards. But I have published, using periods of unemployment the way you use sabbaticals.

You tell me I don't have the appropriate terminal degree for a position in English.

I took an American Studies degree back when interdisciplinary scholarship was in vogue, the way multi-culturalism (whatever it is you mean by that) is now. Since then, I have taught English, studied American literature, and published in literary journals. But you're not satisfied; my application goes into the pile of "other." If you can't find an English Ph.D., then you consider mine. I was taught that the true scholar was self-taught. I was taught that one's true education began after graduate school. You may say that, but you don't believe it.

You said I could be your part-time lover.

You offered me four-sections of composition, an eighty percent load, and you offered to pay me half of what a full-time beginning instructor receives. You also offered to let me teach at other schools to supplement my income, schools which would follow your example and pay by the course credit. That was in the fall; in the spring you might not need me. In the spring, I can sit at home and wait for you to call.

You tell me I've never taught the particular course you want taught.

Did you read my application? When one teaches overseas, one gives up the notion of specialties. I have taught phonetics, art history, American history, Shakespeare, American literature, the history of criticism, world civilization and a dozen or more other courses. Teaching overseas is like a career of pinch-hitting; one is always filling in for the faculty member who didn't return from her vacation. Did you ever consider flexibility as a job criterion?

You don't like my letters.

Sometimes you don't respond at all, or you tell me that you will not be responding unless you wish me to pursue my suit. Sometimes you tell me that you have decided not to take a new suitor this new year. Always you respond with a form letter. And, oh, the letters you send. Sometimes you mix up your envelopes and send me a letter meant for someone else. Most of the time you tell me others are better suitors; they more closely met your requirements. (I often have the sense that you have not been honest about just what your requirements are.) Often you tell me that my name will be kept on file, but I know that this too is rarely true. Frequently you tell me that I have impressive credentials, but you are not impressed. Worse, sometimes you tell me what a fine job your committee did in hiring someone else. Still worse, sometimes you tell me all about the fine qualifications of your chosen one. (And I have recognized a few bounders among them.) But you almost always thank me for my interest in you.

Well, enough. The last right (rite) of the spurned lover is to say farewell. Goodbye. I won't be bothering you any more. Like many another spurned lover, I am going away, as far as I can get.

Farewell to Teaching

by Jody Lannen Brady

C ollege teaching, in my experience, bears little relation to the fairy tale ivory tower parents hope they're buying when they hock everything to pay today's astronomical tuition bills.

After twelve years of teaching college writing, I have taught my last class. I said I was going to quit several times before, so I had become a little like Peter calling "Wolf," and my family and friends stopped listening. But I mean it this time—I'm not going back—and I feel compelled to tell anyone willing to listen why I have left teaching.

I began teaching without any understanding of what I was setting out to do. I was a graduate student in a writing program and needed the money a teaching assistantship gave me. I began tutoring in the Writing Center the same semester I took my one and only teaching class with an instructor who was subsequently fired. The class read the instructor's doctoral dissertation, kept a journal and "shared" our writing with one another. That was my preparation to teach.

For a year, I felt my way through the process of spontaneously responding to pieces of writing. A student would come in for an appointment; we sat at a table and read the student's writing, and then I offered advice on what the student needed to re-work. Before I sat down the first day to give this writing advice, I had never thought about teaching or how I wrote or what constituted good writing or how one got from the tangled scrawl of a first draft to a polished piece of writing.

If you're feeling sorry for the students who I learned on, just wait. It gets worse. Around the time I started feeling competent in my tutoring, my assignment was switched, and I was given writing classes. Twenty-two freshmen per class—fresh out of high school and full of expectations and anxiety.

The first thing I discovered was that a writing course could quickly become a confessional. Students turned in "papers" that were run-on rants against their parents, that spilled out the tangled details of date rape and friends' suicides, that confessed fears about sexual orientation. I could suggest the need for organization and concrete detail, and I could underline awkward phrasing and circle comma splices. But I was unprepared to deal with the emotional needs expressed in the writing.

I did my learning on the job. I read fewer "confessions" once I learned to hand out information early in the semester about professional counseling services available on campus, and once I learned to clarify the concepts of audience and purpose. I fiddled with how much to have students write and what to have them read, how much group work and how many comments on drafts. I spent hours and hours at home sweating out grading decisions, and I attempted to carry off a breezy, informal in-class presence.

I had good semesters and bad semesters in the beginning—caused by a mix of class chemistry, syllabus experimentation, fluctuating university policy and demands on my time. Over time, the ups and down settled into a more steady course of teaching, a balance between what was good for my students and what was good for me.

I shared a dingy office with twenty other instructors, and some semesters I was lucky to find a chair to perch on during my office hours. I often met with students in the hallway because it was quieter than the office. I had one file cabinet drawer I could call my own, but I hauled all my papers and books back and forth from home to office and back each day because I couldn't work in the office, never knowing how many times I would have to jump up and answer the phone, and if I would have a desk to sit at. Ironically, once I was on my way out the door, they found money to remodel the office, and it's no longer the depressing pit it was for all the years I sat in it.

Because I was a lecturer, I was paid by the class—whether I taught sixteen students or twenty-six. In a writing class, each student in the classroom translates into hours of individual attention, most of it spent responding to writing assignments—so the number of students in a class had a great deal to do with how I felt about my compensation. Early on, I gave into student pleas to overload my courses. Over time, I developed the thick skin needed to say, "no" as many times as necessary to keep a class maxed at twenty-two students, but classes can be hard to come by, and I never managed to get past feeling bad about saying "no."

I learned to keep my classes as small as possible, to get more efficient in my grading, to gauge a reasonable work load for a class and to focus on a few areas, which help the majority of novice writers. Consequently, I got over most of my deep-seated fear of being discovered for the fraud I felt I was. I was, after all, a writer of no great success who spent more time telling people how to write than I spent writing myself.

My frustrations with teaching came from all these things: from lack of training, from self-doubt, from being paid poorly, from having no place to call my own, from bad time management—and from a system of labor exploitation.

Administrators have learned what a bargain hired hand educators are. We get paid a fraction of a full-timer's salary, and we get no benefits, almost no administrative support, and no employment guarantees. In exchange, we teach many of the same classes as full-time faculty and do a lot of uncompensated work for the university. Sounds like a hard deal to resist.

I was a bad guest at a reception for the new president of the university. I took advantage of the receiving line and, after introducing myself, I went into a spiel about how I hoped he would make teaching his top priority and would take look at the deplorable teaching conditions of lecturers at the university.

I expected a sage nod and a little more—but I didn't even get that.

"That's a problem everywhere I've been," he told me. "It's not our problem."

I moved on to let the next person say hello, and I shook hands with the president's wife and moved on out of the way, all the while hearing his response echo in my head. How—I wanted to ask him—does the fact that the problem is widespread make it not a problem? How can you dismiss the problem so glibly when you've just told me that you're aware of it?

I knew at that moment that this president had given me the last push out the door that I'd been waiting for.

Leaving teaching has not been an easy decision for me. Besides the obvious fears that come with losing my only steady paycheck, I lost my students. I like working with students, and most of the time, I like listening to them. I like learning from them. I know that I've learned more about writing from my students than I have from any writing teacher I ever encountered as a student myself.

In order to grade papers, I have had to crystallize what makes writing effective and what makes writing weak. In order to teach, I have read wonderful books about writing that I never would have picked upon my own. I give my students advice about writing, and then I feel compelled to follow it myself—to carry my notebook around, to write every day, to stay loose in my first draft, to listen for my own voice, to revise ambitiously and to edit ruthlessly.

I miss all this. I miss the camaraderie of the classroom. I miss the joy of reading something wonderful from a student who thought he or she couldn't write anything worthwhile.

But the president—without possibly being able to understand what his words would mean to me—told me that I could count on another twelve years of all the same frustrations if I stayed. He might have come into the university talking about the quality of education provided by the university, but on my way out, I understood him to say, "You part-time teachers don't matter."

Though tenure line faculty teach only 39% of the courses in this English Department, they are still the only educators who anyone appears to have in mind when they talk about the quality of education. Part-time, low-paid workhorse faculty are still invisible.

I could stay and join the fight of part timers slaving away in committee rooms and conferences, but I walked away from the fight because I don't share the optimism of my crusading peers. I don't believe that administrators have any intention of addressing the concerns of their part-time employees; as long as there are over-qualified teachers willing to fill low-cost positions, there's little incentive to change.

So, I'm staying home this semester for the first time in twelve years, and I wish all the best to the students I won't meet—and to the invisible teacher who signed a contract to teach my classes.

ABOUT THE CONTRIBUTORS

Kathryn Albrecht has taught at a number of prisons as well as in other community colleges, and she believes that teaching in a correctional institution brings specific challenges and rewards.

Jody Lannen Brady taught writing classes for twelve years at George Mason University in Fairfax, Virginia. Currently, she is a freelance writer. Her stories have appeared in journals and anthologies, including *A More Perfect Union: Poems and Stories about the Modern Wedding* (St Martin's Press, 1999). "Farewell to Teaching" was originally published in *American Jones Building & Maintenance.*

Diana Claitor taught writing skills and tutored students in developmental writing and English at Austin Community College but quit because of the working conditions and low pay. A longtime journalist, editor and researcher, she is now an editor for Wexford Publishing and writes fiction.

Elayne Clift is a writer in Saxtons River, Vermont. Currently she teaches at Vermont College, the University of Vermont and Keene (NH) State College. She is the author of several books, more recently a memoir *To New Jersey with Love and Apologies* (OGN, 1999).

Peggy de Broux, a native of West Texas, has been writing poetry since the mid 1980s. She has been published in a variety of journals and co-edited a chapbook entitled *I Say No to Rape*. She is the 1995 recipient of the Naomi Clark Scholarship from Centrum, the Port Townsend Writer's Conference and has won a poetry prize at the Olympic Literary Workshop. She has taught English and French, taught creative writing and done readings of her own work at various sites in Port Angeles and Port Townsend, Washington.

Cynthia Duda has had her work published in *North Shore Sunday, Street Smarts, Poetpourri, The Anthology of New England Writers, The Monadnock Review,* and *The Atlanta Review.* She is a graduate of the Vermont College MFA program and has taught writing in the Boston area.

Brigitte Dulac has taught French for twenty years in community colleges and at a university where she also taught a course in literary translations. Her students' translations were published in three consecutive books, which she edited. Some of her short stories and poems have been published in American and Franco-American literary magazines. One of the short stories was translated and reprinted in Germany. One French poem, published in a French journal, brought her the title of Poet Laureate for the year.

Kate Gale is an English instructor at four colleges and two universities. Her three published books are *Blue Air, Where Crows and Men Collide* and *Water Moccasins.* She has had numerous poems published in a variety of literary journals including *Arshile, Bakunin, Portland Review* and *The Northeast Journal.* She has recently edited a short story collection called *Anyone Is Possible* for Red Hen Press, where she now works as a contributing editor.

Andrew Guy remains an adjunct instructor. He regularly gives papers at conferences and publishes essays in academic journals and anthologies. As a fiction writer, he has been awarded residency at the MacDowell Colony and been nominated for a Pushcart Prize. Andrew Guy is a pen name.

Barbara Wilson Hahn was born in Sharon, Pennsylvania in 1941. Following graduation, she attended Thiel College in Greenville, Pennsylvania, where she received her B.A. in Medical Technology in 1964. She worked for 30 years as a board-certified Medical Technologist (MT-ASCP) in various hospital and clinic laboratories in Pennsylvania, Colorado, Louisiana and Arizona. In the mid 1980s, she was accepted into the graduate degree program at Northern Arizona University where she received her Master's in English in 1990. As an adjunct instructor in the English Department, she subsequently taught creative writing for a few semesters at a local community college. She now divides her time between doing lab work, teaching writing workshops, writing novels, and maintaining a ten-acre ranch in Cornville, Arizona. In March of 2000, her novel *A Race for Glory* was accepted for publication by AmErica House Publishers.

Kathleen Burk Henderson is an essayist, poet and writing consultant living in Dallas, Texas. She is a 1999 Pushcart Prize Nominee, and Guest Editor of Volume 3, Number 1 (Summer 2000) of *The Melic Review* (www.melicreview.com). "From the Shade of the Tower" first appeared in *Savoy Magazine* (www.savoy.net).

Gary P. Henrickson holds a B.A., an M.A. and a Ph.D. from the University of Minnesota. He is a Vietnam veteran. He has taught in North Yemen, Syria, Poland, Taiwan and Russia, and he is currently Associate Professor and Chair of the Department of English and Humanities at North Dakota State College of Science. He has published academic articles and fiction in a variety of journals. He has adapted parts of *Huckleberry Finn* for the stage. He is currently at work on a comic novel set in Russia, *The Budgie Factor.* "A Lover's Complaint" was written when the author was between jobs.

Will MacKenzie came to teaching because he does it well and not because he had planned it. His family has no record of him expressing a desire to be a teacher; they wanted a physician. At seven, he had toyed with the idea of becoming an explorer like Thor Heyerdal. His adult career began in the U.S. Navy, first as a swabbie, then after the Naval Academy, a commission in the surface fleet. For a shore tour, he elected to teach. From there it was out of the Navy to the Harvard Graduate School of Education, then Clark University. He currently teaches at two universities in New England and consults on technology in education.

Anesa Miller holds a Ph.D. from the University of Kansas. She is editor/translator of *Re-Entering the Sign: Articulating New Russian Culture* (University of Michigan Press, 1995) and *After the Future: The Paradoxes of Postmodernism and Contemporary Russian Culture* (The University of Massachusetts Press, 1995). She has also published a book of poetry titled *A Road Beyond Loss*. Most recently, her fiction has appeared in *Cimarron Review*, the *Cream City Review* and *The Kenyon Review*.

Ed Meek teaches English and does freelance writing.

Martin Naparsteck has taught at nine colleges in three states and has long been active in trying to improve conditions for part-time faculty. He has been fired from two of those colleges because of his activities. He has written two novels, *War Song* and *A Hero's Welcome* and thirty short stories. He lives in Rochester, New York and is the book reviewer for the *Salt Lake Tribune*.

Jim Neal describes himself as a modern-day Ichabod Crane and has vowed to never teach more than six classes a semester again.

John D. Nesbitt worked as an adjunct instructor at two community colleges, one state university and two UC campuses, all in California, before finding a full-time position at Eastern Wyoming College, where he has been teaching for nineteen years. He has published a wide variety of articles, short stories, poems and books. His most recent book is *Coyote Trail*, a Western novel. Some of his own classroom ghosts are suppressed in his *Blue Book of Basic Writing* as well as in a short story and poem here and there.

R. Piehler (of necessity a pseudonym) teaches Art History at several small colleges in the greater New York area.

J. L. Schneider was a carpenter for fifteen years before becoming an adjunct professor of English at Dutchess Community College in Poughkeepsie, New York. His fiction has appeared in a variety of publications.

M. Theodore Swift recently realized he will likely never get a full-time job in higher education and must do something else. He wants a career that will bring him more money, security and respect than being a college teacher ever did, and so he is currently debating over becoming a garbage collector, a grave digger or a pornographer.

Edward Tassinari was born in the Bronx and lives in Scarsdale, New York. He has a B.A. in American History, an M.A. in Latin American History and a Ph.D. in Inter-American Studies. Besides teaching history, his interests, scholarly and otherwise, include the role of sports in American society, chess, film noir and the 1950s. He has published articles in a variety of publications. He is presently teaching American History on the college level.

Dr. Kathleen Joy Tigerman earned her M.A. and her Ph.D. from the University of Wisconsin-Milwaukee and has taught in the University of Wisconsin system for seventeen years. She won a teacher of the year award from the students at a two-year UW college. After seven years as an adjunct at the University of Wisconsin-Platteville where she teaches currently, she was hired into a tenure-track position but given no time towards tenure. In 2001, the University of Wisconsin Press will publish her book *Wisconsin Indian Literature: Anthology of Native Voices*.

Tim Waggoner has published over fifty short stories and hundreds of non-fiction articles. After eleven years as an adjunct, he is now a full-time, tenure-track assistant professor of English at Sinclair Community College in Dayton, Ohio.

Erica Werner is in a state of transition. She has temporarily left the teaching profession but misses the work very much. She continues to work full-time for the U.S. Postal Service. She lives in Birmingham, Alabama with her four dogs and assorted other pets. She has just completed a screenplay.

Paul Yovino is a communications and public relations professional who has worked in both fields for the last fifteen years. He was Media Director of *BH&M Advertising and Public Relations* in Boston and Executive Producer of *The Jerry Williams Talk Program* on WRKO Radio. He had his own daily talk program, *The Paul Yovino Program*, on WMRE Radio in Boston. He has been a lecturer and adjunct instructor at several colleges and universities in the Boston Area. He is currently working with the new WMEX Talk Radio station in a marketing capacity. He graduated from Thayer Academy in Braintree and earned a B.A. Degree from the University of Massachusetts in Political Science and Journalism. He attended Suffolk University Law School and Boston University's Graduate School of Communication. He is the author of the book *A Case of Summary Judgement*, which recounts some of his experiences in the broadcasting industry. He lives in Milton, Massachusetts.

About the Contributors

Michael Dubson has an A.A. from Parkland College, a B.A. and an M.A. from the University of Massachusetts and a graduate certificate from Emerson College. He has been an author, an editor, a journalist and an actor. He has taught Developmental Writing, Freshman Composition, Literature and Journalism at a number of greater Boston colleges, primarily in the Massachusetts state community college system. In 2000, one of his students nominated him to be a member of Who's Who in American College Teachers. He has become an activist in the struggle to improve working conditions for adjunct faculty. It was his own experiences as an adjunct that inspired him to compile this collection.

ORDER FORM

Additional copies of *Ghosts in the Classroom* can be ordered directly from the publisher.

NAME _____

ADDRESS_____

CITY _____

STATE_____ZIP _____

DAYTIME TELEPHONE:(_____)_____

Please send _____ copies of *Ghosts in the Classroom* at $12.95 per copy ($10.00 per copy for orders of 5 or more). Please add $2.00 per order for postage and handling. Massachusetts residents please add 5% sales tax.

Mail to: Camel's Back Books, Box 181126, Boston, Massachusetts 02118

Enclosed is $_____ in

_____ Check

_____ Money Order

_____Credit Card   ___Visa   ___Mastercard
                             ___ Discover   ___Am. Exp.

Account Number_____Ex . Date _____

Authorized Signature_____
.

Using your credit card, you can also order by phone or from our website.

1-866-ADJUNCT   **www.camelsbackbooks.com**